Dedication

To George Fortune (1915 – 2012), who played a central role in establishing a standard Shona orthography.

Karen and Mick

Hayden Eastwood and Petros Nkondo

Learning Shona

Functional to Intermediate in 10 lessons

love from Larissa x

The House of Books
Harare 2017

First published in Zimbabwe by
The House of Books
8 Redhill Road, Highlands
Harare, Zimbabwe

ISBN 978-0-7974-8060-5

Production and Editorial
Dimitrije Unkovski

Illustration by
Farai Wallace

Graphic Designer
Dunja Pantic (*www.thedunja.com*)

Printing and Binding
Cicero Ltd
Belgrade, Serbia

Contents

Introduction

This book is designed for students who have mastered the first book of the series, "Learning Shona: Zero to functional in 12 lessons", and who are now looking for a way to take their skills to the next level.

This book assumes that the student has absorbed the majority of material from the first book. Where deemed necessary, however, a brief reminder of previous material is given.

This learning guide is divided into 10 lessons, each of which will take you through a crucial component of the language. You will learn about:

1. Adjectives (important in describing nouns you'll have learned in the first book),
2. Locatives (which will help you to better discuss where things are),
3. Complex use of tenses (which will help you talk more confidently about when things have happened),
4. Active and passive verbs (which will improve your ability to discuss what events are happening to which people)
5. Verb extensions (which are a crucial aspect of speaking Shona fluently)
6. Conjunctions (which will allow you to join complex ideas together)

Towards the end of the book we will look at a wide variety of "miscellane ous" language practices that will prepare you for the large number of idiosyncracies and particular ways of saying things that English speakers often stumble with.

Finally, we'll examine a wide variety of simulated situations that put the above lessons into practice, and which will hopefully provide you with the vocabulary and phrasing to navigate similar situations.

Congratulations on progressing to the intermediate stage of learning. Shona is a challenging language but, as I'm sure you will agree, both fascinating and satisfying once you have the hang of it. Good luck with getting to the next level of proficiency!

Lesson 1

ADJECTIVES

Adjectives

In Lesson 9 of the first book of the series, "Zero to Functional in 12 Lessons" we looked at how to correctly use Shona nouns in sentences. Here we build on this base by examining how to describe nouns with actual adjectives.

In English an adjective is always placed **before** the noun (as in the sentence, "the good boy") whereas in Shona it is always placed **after** the noun.

There are three kinds of adjectives in Shona: "Ordinary", "stative", and "English-numerical". "Ordinary adjectives" follow the standard rules of noun agreement (discussed below). "Stative adjectives" differ to ordinary adjectives in that they derive from Shona verbs. "English-numerical" adjectives, in contrast to both other classes, derive from English words.

The above three adjective classes have their respective differences, but they all share the common motif of having to agree with the nouns they pair with.

How noun agreements work

A "noun prefix" is the first 2-3 letters of a noun that indicates its noun-grouping. For example, the prefix of "murume" (man) is "**mu**", the prefix of "**chi**bage" (maize) is "**chi**" and the prefiz of "**dzi**mbwa" (dogs) is "**dzi**". In each case the prefixes, "**mu**", "**chi**" and "**dzi**", indicate that the nouns are grouped as "human", "universal" and "soft-sounding" (plural), respectively[1] (Figure 1).

The prefix (and corresponding noun-grouping) are important because they indicate how the adjective should agree with the verb, as is now explained for the three adjective classes.

[1] If this is baffling, please refer to Lesson 9 of Learning Shona: Zero to Functional in 12 Lessons, which extensively introduces nouns and how to make them agree with verbs.

***Figure 1**. A reminder of noun-groupings from the first book in the series. Recall that nouns are split into human and non-human groupings. Non-human nouns can themselves be subdivided into hard-sounding, soft-sounding, universal and trees (often known as "mu/mi").*

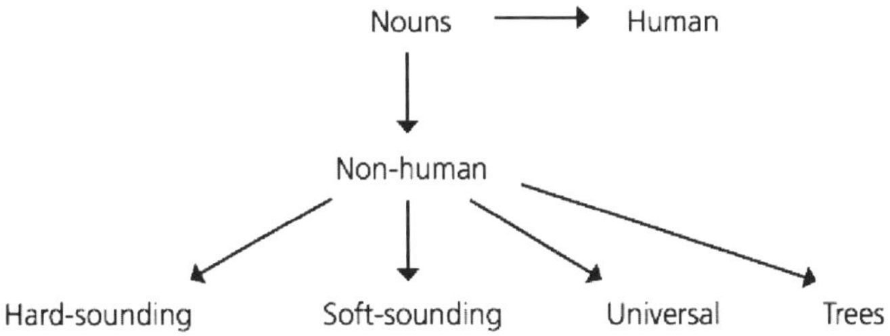

Ordinary adjectives

An ordinary adjective agrees with a noun by taking on the noun's prefix, as the rule below demonstrates:

Rule: Using urdinary adjectives
Noun + noun-prefix + adjective
Eg. **mu**rume + "**mu**" + "pfupi" = **mu**rume **mu**pfupi (the short man)

The most common "ordinary" adjectives are shown below (Table 1):

***Table 1**. Common "ordinary" adjectives*

Adjective (Shona)	**Adjective (English)**
pfupi,	short,
guru,	big,
tete,	thin,
gobvu,	fat,
diki,	small,
refu.	tall/long.

Conjugating adjectives with the "human" noun class

Recall that humans are described by nouns prefixed with "mu" or "va"[2]. Below are some examples of ordinary adjectives describing the human class in its singular and plural form:

Singular (mu)	**Plural (va)**
mukomana **mu**diki a small boy	**va**komana **va**diki small boys
musikana **mu**diki a small girl	**va**sikana **va**diki small girls
murume **mu**diki a small man	**va**rume **va**diki small men
mukadzi **mu**diki a small woman	**va**kadzi **va**diki small women

Conjugating adjectives with the "non-human" noun class

As previously mentioned, there are 5 types of non-human nouns, as outlined in Figure 2: "hard sounding", "soft sounding", "universal", and "trees" (also known as "mu/mi") (Figure 2).

***Figure 2**. Non-human noun groupings*

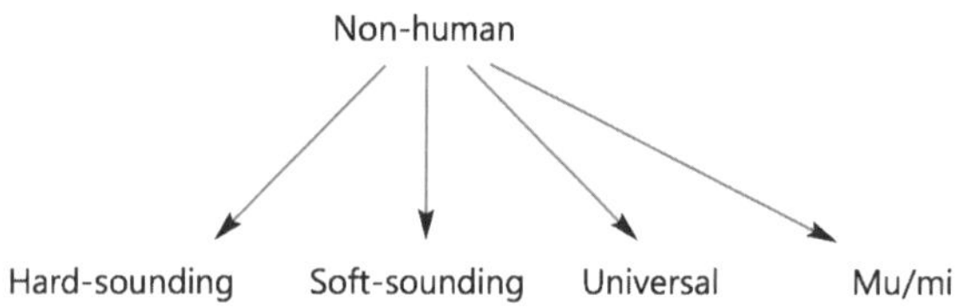

[2] All human nouns begin with "mu" or "va" except for certain "honoured" people, such as, grandfather (sekuru), grandmother (ambuya), father (baba) and mother (amai), as discussed in "Zero to functional in 12 lessons".

Ordinary conjugations of each of these noun grouping are discussed below.

Hard sounding nouns

Nouns beginning with: "b", "d", "g", "j", "r" and "z" signal that nouns fall into the "hard-sounding" group[3].

Hard sounding nouns in the singular form do not have a prefix and, as such, the adjectives that describe them, likewise, have no prefix.

Hard-sounding nouns pluralise with the prefix "ma" and, therefore, the adjective in the plural form agrees with this:

Singular (mu)	**Plural (va)**
badza guru a big hoe	**ma**padza **ma**kuru big hoes
dhorobha guru a big town	**ma**dhorobha **ma**kuru big towns
gudo guru a big baboon	**ma**kudo **ma**kuru big baboons
jira guru a big cloth	**ma**chira **ma**kuru big cloths
rize guru a big scorpion	**ma**rize **ma**kuru big scorpions
zai guru a big egg	**ma**zai **ma**kuru big eggs

Note, above, that "g" turns to "k" when words like "guru" are pluralised. This is because the "k" is slightly easier to pronounce in the plural than the "g" and, therefore, as is often the case in languages like French and Shona,

[3] Recall that the word "sadza" is an exception and is always conjugated as though it is hard-sounding (despite the fact that it should be classified as "soft", owing to it beginning with an "s").

subtle changes are made to the pronunciation to make the language "flow" better.

Soft-sounding nouns

Words that begin with "f", "h", "i", "k", "m", "p" and "s" (except for when referring to "sadza") and "w" denote "soft-sounding" nouns. This noun class has no prefix in either the singular or the plural form and, as such, "ordinary" adjectives describing them are, likewise, characterized by the absence of a prefix:

Singular (mu)	**Plural (va)**
foshoro guru[4] a big hoe	foshoro guru big hoes
nyoka guru a big snake	nyoka guru big snakes
mbavha guru a big thief	mbavha guru big thieves
kitsi guru a big cat	kitsi guru big cats

Universal conjugations

Words beginning with the prefix "chi" or "zvi" denote the "universal" noun group. The same example, "guru", below, shows some "ordinary adjective" conjugations, using the same principle:

[4] Note, above, that the only way someone can know that a "big hoe" is being referred to rather than "big hoes", is through specifying further information. Someone would have to, for example, say more about the hoe (or hoes): "foshoro guru **yaka**bvisa ivhu" (the big shovel removed the soil), or "foshoro guru **dzaka**bvisa ivhu" (the big shovels removed the soil).

Singular (mu)

chipo **chi**kuru
a big gift

chipatara **chi**kuru
a big hospital

chinhu **chi**kuru
a big thing

chiso **chi**kuru
a big face

chiroto **chi**kuru
a big dream

Plural (va)

zvipo **zvi**kuru
big gifts

zvipatara **zvi**kuru
big hospitals

zvinhu **zvi**kuru
big things

zviso **zvi**kuru
big faces

zviroto **zvi**kuru
big dreams

Mu/mi conjugations

Words beginning with the prefix "mu/mi" denote the "mu/mi" group and most often describe trees, vegetables and, for some reason known only to the Gods, certain parts of the body. Once again the verb "guru" illustrates the agreement procedure:

Singular (mu)

muchero **mu**kuru
a big fruit

muti **mu**kuru
a big tree

muriwo **mu**kuru
a big vegetable

muromo **mu**kuru
a big mouth

muviri **mu**kuru
a big body

Plural (va)

michero **mi**kuru
big fruit (plural)

miti **mi**kuru
big trees

miriwo **mi**kuru
big vegetables

miromo **mi**kuru
big mouths

miviri **mi**kuru
big bodies

musoro **mu**kuru
a big head

misoro **mi**kuru
big heads

Stative adjectives

A stative adjective is an adjective that refers to a noun in a state of being (ie describing a characteristic that is presumed to be long-lasting or permanent).

Stative adjectives are formed from verbs that have been converted into their past tense form (and this is true for both Shona and English).

In English, a good example of a stative adjective is the word "enchanted". In the sentence, "the enchanted forest", the verb "enchant" is used in its past tense form ("enchanted") to describe the present state of a particular forest. Other examples of stative sentences in English include:

He is seated (using the past tense, of "seat")
She is annoyed (using the past tense of "annoy")
The boys are tired (using the past tense of "tire")

The rule box, below, explains the use of stative adjectives.

Rule: Using stative adjectives
Noun + past tense conjugation + verb
Eg. **mu**rume + **"aka"** + "dzidza" = **mu**rume **aka**dzida (the learned man)

The following examples show the rule in action. Note that the noun must agree **not** with the noun prefix (as is the case with "ordinary" adjectives), but with the **past tense form of the verb (Table 1)**:

***Table 1**. A reminder of past tense agreements for the different noun-groupings*

	human	**soft**	**hard**	**universal**	**mu/mi**
Singular	aka	yaka	raka	chaka	waka
Plural	vaka	dzaka	aka	zvaka	yaka

Singular (mu)

muchero **waka**tsvuka
red [ripe] fruit

Plural (va)

michero **yaka**tsvuka
ripe fruit (plural)

murume **aka**tsvuka
the red [pale] man

varume **vaka**tsvuka
red [pale] men

chipikiri **chaka**tsvuka
a red (or rusty) nail

zvipikiri **zvaka**tsvuka
red (or rusty) nails

imba **yaka**tsvuka
a red house

dzimba **dzaka**tsvuka
red houses

gudo **raka**tsvuka
a red baboon

makudo **aka**tsvuka
red baboons

Commonly used stative verbs include:

Verb	**Eg with stative adjective**
"-naka" "be good"	musikana wakanaka beautiful girl
"-ora" "be off"	mazai akaora rotten eggs
"-biwa" "be stolen"	motokari dzakabiwa stolen cars
"-pusa" "easy/stupid"	murume akapusa stupid man
"-tyoka" "break"	bhasikoro rakatyoka broken bicycle
"-kora" "be thick"	mapango akakora thick planks
"-onda" "be thin"	vakadzi vakaonda thin women
"-oma" "be dry/difficult"	basa rakaoma difficult work

"English numerical" adjectives

In Shona, English is often used to describe numerical quantities. In this case, there is no conjugation or agreement, per se, but a rule that the English number be placed immediately after the noun. For example, "1 person" would translate with the above rationale to "munhu one" and "2 people" would translate to "vanhu two".

Rule: Using stative adjectives
Noun + English number
Eg. murume + "**1**" = murume **1** (one man)

The following examples apply the rule:

Singular	**Plural**
vhiki 1 one week	mavhiki 2 2 weeks
chiremba 1 1 doctor	vanachiremba 4 4 doctors
zai 1 1 egg	mazai 12 12 eggs
katsi 1 1 cup	katsi 5 5 cats
mudzi 1 1 root	midzi 7 7 roots
chingwa 1 one [loaf of] bread	zvingwa 8 8 [loaves of] bread

Exercises

1. For the following adjectives write down the adjective stem used:
    a. (Example) muchero mudiki, Answer: **diki**
    b. (Example) michero mikobvu. Answer: **kobvu**
    c. Huku guru
    d. Mikaka mishoma
    e. Shumba gobvu
    f. Vakomana varefu
    g. Mukadzi mutete
2. Fill in the correct prefix in the following sentences:
    a. Eg. mubiki **mu**pfupi
    b. Musikana _refu
    c. Chibage __tsvuku
    d. Mhuka __zhinji
    e. Badza __dema
    f. Makomo _tete
3. Place the correct pronoun in the following sentences for the stative adjective, "naka":
    a. Eg. Mukomana **waka**naka
    b. Mbudzi ____naka (singular)
    c. Michero ___naka
    d. Chingwa __naka
    e. Gomba ___naka
    f. Zviso ___naka
    g. Nguruve ___naka (plural)
    h. Makudo ___naka
4. Translate the following passage into English:
   Rimwe zuva mukomana mudiki akaenda kuchipatara. Akati kunaDokota varefu, "ndine musoro". Dokota vakabvunza kune mukomana, "wakatanga kurwadza rini?" Mukomana akati, "wakatanga pandakadonha mugomba rakadzika." Dokota akati, "ndinoda kuita X-ray, asi machine ye-X-ray yakafa. Saka, iyezvino ndichakupa mapiritsi akatsvuka 2."

Vocabulary list

-biwa	stolen
-dzidza	learn
-dzika	reduce
-kora	thick
-naka	good
-onda	thin
-ora	bad/rotten
-pusa	easy
-rize	sting/bite
-rwadza ne	in pain of [something]
-rwara	sick
-ti	say
-tsvuka	be red/ripe
-tyoka	break
badza	hoe
chingwa	bread
chinhu	thing
chipatara	hospital
chipikiri	nail
chipo	gift
chiremba	doctor
chiroto	dream
chiso	face
dhorobha	town
diki	small (adjective)
foshoro	shovel
gobvu	thick
gomba	ditch
gudo	baboon
guru	big (adjective)
huku	chicken
imba	house
jira	cloth
kitsi	cat

mbavha	thief
mbudzi	goat
muchero	fruit
mudzi	root
mukadzi	woman
mukaka	milk
mukomana	boy
muriwo	vegetables
muromo	mouth
murume	man
musikana	girl
musoro	head
muti	tree
muviri	body
nguruve	pig
nyoka	snake
pfupi	short (adjective)
refu	tall (adjective)
rimwe	another (hard sounding conjugation)
shumba	lion
tete	aunt
zai	egg

Lesson 2

LOCATIVES

Locatives

In English, the standard locatives "at", "to" and "in" communicate where things (or people) are. When talking about places in English, "to" is usually more "general" than "at". So, for example, we talk about going "to town" (because town is a general place) but we talk about being "at a friend's house" (because a friend's house is a concrete location rather than a general vicinity).

In Shona, location is similarly expressed with degrees of location certainty, though far more rigorously than in English.

Nearby things

In Shona, the "closest" locative is "pa". It describes something within your immediate visible vicinity, or, alternatively, a very specific location. For example, "I am at home", is an example of a specific location in English, which translates to "ndiri **pa**mba" in Shona. Some further examples of this locative are shown in the table below:

Shona	English
akagara **pa**chigaro **pa**nze[5]	he is seated on the chair outside
muri **pa**chitoro	you are at the store
uri **pa**dhuzi	you are close by
zviri **pa**si	those things are on the ground
arikutaura **pa**phone	he/she is talking on the phone

Referring to more distant things

When referring to more general places in Shona, the locative "ku" is used (this is the same "ku" that is used in verb infinitives, but it also refers to *general* locations). For example, "I went to town" translates to "ndakaenda **ku**taundi".

[5]Note that when discussing "outside" using "-nze", that both "ku" (making "kunze") and "pa" (making "panze") are equally valid.

Further examples of general locations:

Shona	English
tinogara **ku**Harare	we live in Harare
baba vanorima **ku**musha	dad farms at the rural homestead
mapurisa ari **ku**mba	the policemen are at the house
musikana akasvika **ku**chikoro kuma 7am	the girl arrived at school at 7am
vanachiremba vakasara **ku**chipatara	the doctors remained at the hospital

Note, above, that the English translation frequently uses "at" or "in", even though the reference to a general vicinity ("ku") is used in the Shona sentence. There is, unfortunately, no clear rule as to when "ku" will translate to "at", "to", or "in" and the beginner is required simply to keep in mind that locatives are used in a stricter way in Shona and that, therefore, a variety of possible translations make sense or "sound right" in English.

Referring to "in" or "inside"

When referring to "in" in Shona, the locative "mu" is used. The following examples show this use more clearly:

Shona	English
ndinogara **mu**Harare	I live in Harare[6]
akasiya sadza **mu**drum	he/she left sadza in the drum
hove dziri **mu**rwizi	the fish are in the river
siyai zvipikiri **mu**bhegi!	leave the nails in the bag!
muchawana map **mu**motokari	you will find the map in the car

If you want to be more precise and say "inside", use "mukati me", as the following examples show:

[6]Note that "ku" and "mu" can be used interchangeably when referring to living in a city or town.

Shona	English
motokari iri **mukati me**workshop	the car is inside the workshop
shiri iri **mukati me**muti	the bird is inside the tree [trunk]
michero iri **mukati me**imba yekutandarira	the fruit is inside the sitting room
resiti iri **mukati me**bhuku	the receipt is inside the book
vatungamirire vari mukati memusan-gano	the leaders are in the middle of a meeting

Locative phrases

Other useful Shona location phrases are shown in the table below. Note that "pe", "ne" and "me" must become "pa", "na" and "ma" when referring to peoples' names, street names and months or years.

PEDYO NE/PADHUZE NE – NEAR TO

Shona	English
pedyo nechitoro	near to the store
pedyo nebhasikoro	near the bicycle
ari **pedyo na**4th street	he/she is near 4th street
tiri **padhuze ne**zvitoro	we are close to the shops we
tichange tiri **padhuze ne**twiza	will be close to the giraffes
Makanga muri **padhuze ne**kufa	you were close to dying
pedyo na Tsitsi	near Tsitsi

PAMUSORO PE – ON TOP OF

Shona	English
pamusoro pe Ngomakurira	on top of Ngomakurira
pamusoro pesherufu	on top of the shelf
pamusoro pa Peter	on top of Peter
pamusoro pa Mavis	on top of Mavis

PASI PE – UNDER

Shona	**English**
pasi petafura	under the table
pasi pekapeti	under the carpet
pasi pa Peter	under Peter
pasi pa Mavis	under Mavis

PAZASI PE – BELOW/BENEATH/AT THE FOOT OF

This phrase is often used interchangeably with "pasi pe", though they are subtly different in meaning.

Shona	**English**
pazasi pegomo	beneath the rock
pazasi pesango	below the forest
pazasi pechitoro	at the foot of the store
pazasi pa Tafadzwa	below Tafadzwa

PASHURE PE – BEHIND [SOMETHING] OR AFTER [DEPENDING ON CONTEXT]

Note that you can use "pashure pe" to refer to both nouns and verbs. When using it with nouns, it means, "behind", and when using it with verbs, it means "after". The table below shows some examples.

Shona	**English**
pashure pemotokari	behind the car
pashure pefafitera	behind the window
pashure pa Rachel	behind Rachel
pashure pekutaura naye	after speaking to him/her
pashure pekugeza ndiro	after washing the dishes
pashure pekupedza basa	after finishing work

MUSHURE ME – AFTER [SOME PERIOD OF TIME]

This is used exclusively when referring to time and in this context, translates to "after [some time]".

Shona	English
mushure me1 hour	after 1 hour
mushure memwedzi mishoma	after a few months
mushure memakore	after some years
mushure mevhiki	after a week

PAMBERI PE – IN FRONT OF, OR AHEAD OF

"Pa" in "pamberi pe" communicates that whatever is "in front" is a few me-tres away. This is in contrast to the case of "kumberi kwe", which will be examined next.

Shona	English
pamberi pe motokari	in front of the car
endai pamberi pemba	go in front of the house
tarisa pamberi pa Monica	look in front of Monica
zvidinha zviri **pamberi pe**tafura	the bricks are in front of the table

KUMBERI KU – IN FRONT OF (BUT FURTHER AWAY THAN THE CASE OF "PA")

The "ku" in "kumberi kwe" communicates that whatever is "in front" is kilometres away, or abstractly "in the distance".

Shona	English
kumberi kwemotokari	way in front of the car
endai kumberi kwemba	go way ahead of the house
tarisa kumberi kwe Monica	look in front of Monica
endai **kumberi ku**svika kuchitoro	Go forward [until] you reach the store

KURE NE – FAR FROM

Shona	English
munofanira kugara **kure ne**mhuka!	You must stay far from the animals!
basa rangu riri **kure ne**dhoroba	My work is far from town
kumusha kwangu **kure ne**rwizi	my [rural] home is far from the river
Ibbo ari **kure na**Vengai	Ibbo is far from Vengai

PANE ["PANA" WHEN REFERRING TO PEOPLE] – AT (OR CLOSE TO)

"Pane/a" translates best to "close by" and can be used interchangeably with "pedyo ne". "Muri pa**na** Scot here?" means "are you near to Scot?" Similarly, "Muri pa**ne** mukaka here?" means, "are you close to the milk?" In the latter example, if we'd left out the "ne" to make "Muri **pa**mukaka here?", this would have translated to "are you on top of the milk?" rather than the intended, "are you close to the milk".

Below are some more examples of using "pane" and "pana"[7] in the context of "near to":

Shona	English
mudhudhudhu uri **pane** motokari	the motorbike is near the car
baba vari **pane** gudo	father is close to the baboon
amai vari **pane** vana	mother is close to the children
mbada dziri **pane** mbudzi	the leopards are close to the goat
foshoro iri **pana** Tendai	the shovel is close to Tendai
ndakanga ndiri **pana** 4th street nezuro	I was close to 4th street yesterday
tichange tiri **pana** chiremba svondo rinouya	we will be close to the doctor next week

[7]Recall that "pa**ne**" should be used when referring to objects and "pa**na**" when referring to people's names or honorific titles and professions.

chingwa chiri **pane** mukaka	the chairs are where the milk is
ayini iri **pane** hembe	the iron is where the shirt is
utsi uri **pane** mudhudhudhu	the smoke is where the motorbike is
Francisca ari **pana** James	Francisca is where James is

PAKATI PE – IN THE MIDDLE OF, BETWEEN

Shona	**English**
pakati pegomo	in the middle of the rock
pakati pemugwagwa	in the middle of the road
pakati pebhuku	in the middle of the book
pakati pemusangano	in the middle of the meeting
imbwa iri **pakati pa**baba nasisi	the dog is between dad and sister

Locating objects (or people) within places

Locatives are often needed when asking questions. For example, "is there someone there?", "how many tools are in here?", "is there any fuel inside that tank, there?"

As a general rule of thumb, use "pa" or "ku" or "mu" on their own when locating places, and "pane", "kune" and "mune" when locating things *within* those places.

For example, "waenda **ku**chikoro here?" translates to "did you go to school?", in which "ku" locates the school. However, if we now want to reference something *within* that school, we must use "kune". For example, "**ku**chikoro, **kune** mabhuku akawanda" translates to "at the school, there are many books".

Note that "kune", above, means "in the vicinity of [some place located by *ku*]".

The examples below show how to refer to places and objects (or people) within those places.

Shona	English
uri padhuze here?	are you close?
ehe, ndiri padhuze	*yes, I'm close*
pagarage **pane** foshoro here?	in the garage is there a shovel?
*ehe, **pa**garage **pane** foshoro*	*yes, in the garage there's a shovel*
uchaisa bepanhau **pa**chigaro here?	will you put the newspaper on the chair?
*ehe, ndichaisa bepanhau **pa**chigaro*	*yes, I'll put the newspaper on the chair*
pane uchi here [pano]?	is there honey [here]?
ehe, pane uchi	*yes, there is honey*
kune mhuka here **ku**Nyanga	are there animals in Nyanga?
ehe, kune mhuka shoma ikoko	*yes, there are a few animals there*
kune zvitoro zvakawanda **ku**Bulawayo here?	are there a lot of shops in Bulawayo?
kwete, hakuna[8] *zvitoro zvakawanda ikoko*	*no, there aren't many shops there*

Information box – When to use "ku" and when to use "pa"
When should you use "ku" to locate something, and when should you use "pa"? This question stumps many students. There is no clear answer, but a general rule of thumb is that, when you're referring to someone, that someone should be in eye-shot for "pa" to be appropriate. When speaking to someone on a phone about something which may be far from you, but close to them, then it's acceptable to use "pa" if the object you're referring to is far from you, but within eye shot of them. Likewise, when discussing one object in relation to another (distance-wise), if they are in "eye-shot" of one another, then use "pa". In all other circumstances, if the object is out of sight of the referencing object (or person) then it's best to keep the locative as "ku".

[8]Don't forget when negating "kune" you must prefix it with "ha" and change the "e" to "a" at the end, to make "hakuna".

QUESTIONS WITH "KU"[9]

Shona	English
uri kuchikoro here?	are you at school?
Ehe, ndiri kuchikoro	*yes, I'm at school*
vari kutaundi here?	are they in town?
kwete, havasi kutaundi. Vari kumba	*no, they're not in town. They're at home*
muchaenda kuSouth Africa here?	are you going to South Africa?
kwete, hatichaenda kuSouth Africa	*no, we're not going to South Africa*
kuGreystone park kunemvura here?[10]	is there water in Greystone Park?
ehe, kune mvura ikoko	*yes, there's water there*
kune mhuka here kuNyanga	are there animals in Nyanga?
ehe, kune mhuka shoma ikoko	*yes, there are a few animals there*
kune zvitoro zvakawanda kuBulawayo here?	are there a lot of shops in Bulawayo?
kwete, hakuna[11] *zvitoro zvakawanda ikoko*	*no, there aren't many shops there.*

QUESTIONS WITH "MU"

Shona	English
muna sekuru here mubathroom?	is there an old man in the bathroom?
ehe, muna sekuru mubathroom	*yes, there is an old man in the bathroom*

---

[9]Note that "ku" can be used to refer to "specific" locations, like a kitchen, in the instance that those specific locations are not in your immediate vicinity. So, for example, if you are close to the kitchen, you should refer to who is in the kitchen using "pa", but if you're far away from it, use "ku".

[10]Note here how "ku" refers to a specific place (Greystone Park) and "kune" refers to water *within* Greystone Park.

[11]Don't forget when negating "kune" you must prefix it with "ha" and change the "e" to "a" at the end, to make "hakuna".

mune zvidzidzo zvipi[12] mubhuku?	what kind of lessons are in the book?
mubhuku mune zvidzidzo memathematics	*in the book there are mathematics lessons*

mumba mune nzara here?	is there hunger in the house?
kwete, hamuna nzara mumba	*no, there is no hunger*

Exercises

1. Choose the correct locative for the following sentences:
   a. Eg. Baba vakagara **pa**chigaro (pa/ku/mu)
   b. Mukomana achaenda ___chitoro (pa/ku/mu)
   c. Murume ari kubika __mba (pa/ku/mu)
   d. Imbwa inorara __nze (pa/ku/mu)
   e. Nhasi ndiri kunzwa __dumbu (pa/ku/mu)
   f. Ndinobva __France (pa/ku/mu)
   g. Tichatora vanhu __chikoro (pa/ku/mu)
   h. _ne mukaka pashelf here? (pa/ku/mu)
2. Translate the following passage into English:
   Nezuro ndakanetswa nemapurisa kutaundi. Ndakabhadhara $20 muripo kuchiteshi chemapurisa. Pashure pekubhadhara ndakaenda kuNyanga. Ndakagara kuMontclair. Zuva iroro ndakaona makudo akawanda netsoko pagomo. Gudo rimwe chete rakapinda mumotokari. Ndakaridzinga asi rakaba mabanana angu pachigaro.

3. Translate the following into Shona:
   Every Monday I collect the children from school. After getting home they eat lunch in the kitchen and then afterwards play outside with their friends. When playing hide and seek they climb trees. Sometimes they fall and scrape their legs. Inside the house there are bandages to put on their wounds. At night they like to sleep near the television.

[12]Note that when the extension "pi" is used with a locative, it means "where", but when it's used with the noun conjugation alone, it means "which". So, for example, "zvidinha zviri ku**pi** ?" means "where are the bricks", but "zvidinha zvi**pi**?" means "which bricks?"

4. Translate the following into Shona:
    a. The rabbit is close to the road
    b. After some days, the car was stolen
    c. The honey is on top of the table
    d. The forest is beneath the mountain
    e. My work is far from home
    f. Is Tendai close to Susan?
    g. Shingi is behind Tapiwa
    h. Inside the cupboard you'll find the pliers
    i. You are close to losing your money

Vocabulary

-ba	steal
-badhara	pay
-donha	fall
-dzinga	chase
-enda	go
-geza	wash
-marwa	scrape
-netswa	bothered by
-nzwa	feel
-pedza	finish
-pinda	enter
-rara	sleep
-rasa	throw away/lose
-rima	plough
-sara	remain
-svika	arrive
-tandarira	socialize
-tarisa	look at
amai	mother
baba	father
bandeji	bandage
bepanhau	newspaper
chidhina	brick
chidzidzo	lesson
chigaro	chair

LOCATIVES

chironda	wound
chiteshi	station
chitoro	store
chivhitivhiti	television
dumbu	stomach/intestines
fafitera	window
gomo	mountain
gore	year
huchi	honey
imba	house
kapeti	carpet
ku	to/at
mbada	leopard
mberi	in front of/forward
mhuka	animal
mu	in
mudhudhudhu	motorbike
mugwagwa	road
mupurisa	policeman
musangano	meeting
mushure me	after
mvura	water
mwedzi	month
ndiro	plate
nhasi	today
pa	on/at
padhuze ne	close to
pakati pe	in the middle of
pamberi pe	in front of
pashure pe	behind
pazasi pe	beneath
pedyo ne	close to
pinjisi	pliers
rwizi	river

Lesson 3

TENSES

Tenses

In the previous book we looked at common tenses, such as the present habitual ("I cook", "I run", "I eat"), present continuous ("I am cooking", "I am running", "I am eating"), and recent and remote past tense ("I ran", "I cooked", "I ate").

We now return to tenses once more and introduce how to communicate complex past events with terms such as, "I was", "I had been", "If only I had", "I used to", "I would have", as well as the more complex future actions, such as "I shall be", "I will be", "I will be having" and "I will have".

The past progressive tense ("was")

The past progressive tense refers to an action that was in the process of happening at some stage in the past. In English this is conveyed by using the word "was". For example, "I was cooking" refers to the action of "cooking" that had been occurring at some previous moment. In effect, the past progressive tense refers to the present continuous tense, but happening in the past.

Because an understanding of the past progressive tense is so dependent on an understanding of the present continuous, we here examine an example of the verb "to cook" in its present continuous form, alongside its Shona equivalent.

We will then look at how to convert this present continuous into its past progressive form.

English	**Shona**
I am cooking	ndiri kubika
you are cooking	uri kubika
he/she is cooking	ari kubika
you (plural) are cooking	muri kubika
we are cooking	tiri kubika
they are cooking	vari kubika

The above present continuous tense is converted into the past progressive tense using "was" to form "I was cooking", "you were cooking", "they were cooking" etc.

The progressive tense in Shona is more complicated than it is in English because it can be created in 1 of 2 ways. Both methods are valid, but one may be more "useful" than another, depending on the context. Which form to use (and when to use it) will become clearer by listening to and conversing with native speakers.

Rule 1 for past progressive tense:

pronoun + "ai"[13] + verb
Eg. ndi + "ai" + "geza" = ndaigeza
I was washing
(but can also mean, depending on the context, "I used to wash")

Rule 2 for past progressive tense

pronoun + past tense[14] + "nga" + pronoun + "ri" + infinitive verb
Eg. ndi + a + "nga" + ndi + "ri" + kugeza = ndanga ndiri kugeza
I was washing [today]

Sometimes people replace "ri" and its infinitve with "chi", though it means the same thing:
pronoun + past tense + "nga" + pronoun + "chi" + verb
Eg. ndi + a + "nga" + ndi + "chi" + geza = ndanga ndichigeza

Examples of the past progressive tense are shown below. In the case of rule 2, only the recent past form is used in order to provide a consistent example.

[13]Note that the infix "ai" can also mean "used to" as well as "was", depending on the context. So "ndaigeza" can mean "I was washing" as well as "I used to wash". We will examine this distinction in more detail later.
[14]Note that the tense can be both recent or remote past depending on whether what's being referred to is today or before.

English	**Shona rule 1 ("ai")**	**Shona rule 2 ("nga")**
I was cooking	ndaibika	ndanga ndiri kubika
you were cooking	waibika	wanga uri kubika
he/she was cooking	aibika	anga ari kubika
you (plural) were cooking	maibika	manga muri kubika
we were cooking	taibika	tanga tiri kubika
they were cooking	vaibika	vanga vari kubika

Now we examine rule 2 in more depth, looking at variations arising from using the remote (rather than the recent) past and the variation of the same, involving "chi". For comparison sake the same verb and pronouns are used below as was used in the previous table.

English	**Shona rule 2 ("ri ku")**	**Shona rule 2 (with "chi")**
I was cooking	ndakanga ndi**ri** **ku**bika	ndakanga ndi**chi**bika
you were cooking	wakanga u**ri** **ku**bika	wakanga u**chi**bika
he/she was cooking	**a**kanga a**ri** **ku**bika	akanga a**chi**bika
you (plural) were cooking	makanga mu**ri** **ku**bika	makanga mu**chi**bika
we were cooking	takanga ti**ri** **ku**bika	takanga ti**chi**bika
they were cooking	vakanga va**ri** **ku**bika	vakanga va**chi**bika

Some further sentences with the past progressive are given below:

Ndaimhanya pandakaona mbavha
I was running when I saw the thief

Ndakanga ndichimhanya pandakaona mbavha
I was running when I saw the thief

Vakanga vari kugeza pakauya vaenzi
They were washing when the visitors arrived

Manga muri kuona chii mu TV?
What were you watching on the TV?

Anga achitaura nani paphone?
Who was he/she speaking to on the phone?

NEGATING THE PAST PROGRESSIVE

Negations for this past tense are similar to the negation rules examined in the first book of this series. In the case of the first rule of the past progressive, involving, "ai" negation is achieved by adding the suffix "sa" to the "ai" stem. The rule below demonstrates this:

Negating the past progressive tense (rule 1)

pronoun + "ai" + "sa" + verb
Eg. ndi + "ai" + "sa"+ "geza" = ndai**sa**geza
I was **not** washing
(but can also mean, depending on the context, "I used **not** to wash")

In the case where "nga" (rule 2) is used for the past progressive tense, the "ri" component is replaced with "si", as the rule below shows:

Negating the past progressive tense (rule 2 – "nga")

pronoun + past tense + "nga[15]" + pronoun + "**si**" + infinitive verb
Eg. ndi + aka[16] + "nga" + ndi + "**si**" + kugeza = ndakanga ndi**si** kugeza

I was **not** washing [yesterday or before]

The above rules are shown in action below, applied to the previous examples:

Ndai**sa**mhanya pandakaona mbavha
I was **not** running when I saw the thief

Ndakanga ndisi kumhanya pandakaona mbavha
I was **not** running when I saw the thief

---

[15]In the case where the alternative form of the past progressive is used (where "ri" substitutes for "chi"), the negation is made by replacing "chi" with "siku".

[16]Note on this occasion that the remote past tense ("aka") was used, but the recent past tense ("a") would have been equally valid (as was the case with the first positive past progressive rule).

Vakanga va**si** kugeza pakauya vaenzi
They were **not** washing when the visitors arrived

Manga mu**si** kuona chii mu TV?
What were you **not** watching on the TV?

Anga a**si** kutaura nani paphone?
Who was he/she **not** speaking to on the phone?

Using "had"

The verb "to have" in English is used everywhere in a variety of tenses. It's important to keep in mind that "had" in Shona is made up of combining the past tense of "to be" with the present tense of "have", as follows:

Rule for "had"

pronoun + tense + "va ne[17]" + noun
Eg. ndi + "a" + "va ne" + mbudzi = nda**va ne**mbudzi
I had a goat [today]

Eg. ndi + "aka" + "va ne" + mbudzi = ndaka**va ne**mbudzi
I had a goat [yesterday or before]

The above rule is shown below in action with some examples, with the present tense provided for comparison sake.

Present tense "have"	Past tense "had"
ndine motokari I have a car	ndaka**va ne**motokari I had a car
tine tafura we have a table	taka**va ne**tafura we had a table
vane mvumo they have permission	vaka**va ne**mvumo they had permission

[17]the "va" component of "ava**ne**" is, in fact, the Shona past tense of the verb "to be". When used with the present tense of the verb "to have" (ie "ne"), it modifies "have" into "had".

mune mhanza
you have luck

maka**va ne**mhanza
you had luck

une motokari itsva
you have a new car

waka**va ne**motokari itsva
you had a new car

NEGATING "HAD" TO "HADN'T" AND "DIDN'T"

In English, the past tense of "have" negates to either "had not" or "did not". For example, the sentence, "I had known" negates to "I hadn't known", but other sentences, like "I had a car" negate to "I didn't have a car".

In Shona, there is no distinction between "hadn't" and "didn't", as the rule below shows:

Rule for negating "had" to "hadn't" and "didn't"

"ha" + pronoun + "na" + "kuva ne" + noun[18]
Eg. "ha" + ndi + "na" + "kuva ne" + mbudzi = **ha**ndi**na kuva ne**mbudzi
I didn't have a goat

The below example illustrates this idea

Past tense "had"	**Negated past tense "hadn't/didn't"**
ndakava nemotokari I had a car	**ha**ndi**na kuva ne**motokari I didn't have a car
takava netafura we had a table	**ha**ti**na kuva ne**tafura we didn't have a table
vakava nemvumo they had permission	**ha**va**na kuva ne**mvumo they didn't have permission
makava nemhanza you had luck	**ha**muna **kuva ne**mhanza you didn't have [any] luck

[18]Note that there is no difference in how the recent and remote past are negated.

wakava nemotokari itsva you had a new car	**ha**una **kuva ne**motokari itsva you didn't have a new car

"I used to"

In English, the term "used to" implies an action that was, at some stage in the past, habitual. We have already seen that "ai", when used with a pronoun, means "was". It can, in Shona, however, also mean "used to". How can we know when it means one or the other? For the most part, "ai" can be though of as "used to" when a specific timeframe has been invoked.

For example: "ndaiverenga", as a sentence on its own, translates to "I was reading", but "Panguva iyoyo ndaiverenga" translates to "at that time, I used to read."

Timeframes that you might use include:

Shona	**English**
panguva iyoyo	during that time
pazororo	during the holidays
pamaweekend	during the weekends
gore rakapera	last year
vhiki rakapera	last week
mwedzi wakapera	last month
muna [year/month]	in [year/month]
mwaka wechando wakapera	last winter

Below are examples of the timeframe in action

"Was"	**"Used to"**
nd**ai**shandisa drill I was using the drill	pazororo, nd**ai**shandisa drill During the holidays I used to use the drill
ini na Tendai t**ai**sekana Tendai and I were laughing at each other	pamaweekend ini naTendai t**ai**sekana on the weekends Tenda and I used to laugh at each other
v**ai**gara vega they used to live alone	muna 2010, v**ai**gara vega In 2010, they used to live alone

John **ai**sevenza kuNandos
John used to work at Nandos

mwedzi wakapera, John **ai**sevenza kuNandos
last month, John used to work at Nandos

m**ai**tamba ne vana kumba
you (plural) were playing with the kids at home

gore rakapera m**ai**tamba vana kumba
during last year, you (plural) used to play with the kids at home

"Will be"/"shall be" ("-nenge/-change") (when discussing actions)

In English people often talk about future states of "present continuous" actions. For example, the sentences, "I will be travelling", "I will be shopping" and "I will be running" all refer to present continuous actions in the future.

The rule below shows the rule for creating the equivalent in Shona:

Rule: "Will" or "shall" (-"nenge" or "-change") (referring to a verb)

pronoun + "nenge" (or "change") + pronoun + "chi" + verb
Eg. ndi + "nenge" + ndi + "chi" buda mumba = ndinenge ndichibuda mumba
Eg. ndi + "change" + ndi + "chi" buda mumba = ndinenge ndichibuda mumba
I will be leaving the house

Further examples of "-nenge" are shown below:

Ndinenge ndichipfeka hembe yangu
I will be wearing my shirt

Anenge achimhanya-mhanya svondo rinouya
He will be rushing this Sunday coming

Vachange vachitakura zvidhinha kumba
They will be carrying the bricks to the house

Tichange tichibika huku mwedzi unouya
We will be cooking chicken next month

Munenge muchikakavadzana naBaba pakunzwa nhau ye corruption yavo
You (plural) will be arguing with father when you hear his corruption story

Ndichange ndichisevenzera kunze kwenyika
I will be working outside the country

"Will be"/"shall be" ("-nenge/-change") (when discussing nouns)

In English, as well as talking about actions that *will be* taking place, it is also common to talk about someone or something being *something*. For example, the sentences, "she will be a doctor", "they will be firemen" and "I will be a priest" all refer to people as different *things*.

In Shona the rule for using the future version of the verb to be, with nouns, is shown below:

Rule: "Will" or "shall" (-"nenge" or "-change") (referring to a noun)

pronoun + "nenge" (or "change") + past pronoun[19] + "va" + noun (or state)
Eg. ndi + "nenge" + nda + "va" = ndinenge ndava chiremba
Eg. ndi + "nenge" + nda + "va" = ndichange ndava chiremba
I will be a doctor

Examples of using the verb "to be" with nouns are given below:

Ndinenge ndava muparidzi
I will be a priest

Unenge wava musoja
You will be a soldier

Tinenge tava vadzidzisi
We will be teachers

Vanenge vava varwere
We will be sick people

[19]The past pronoun is used here but does not refer to anything having occurred in the past.

Conditionals

A conditional, as the name suggests, talks about an event that is (or will be, or was) predicated on the occurrence of some other event. In English conditionals are provided by using "would" or "would have been".

For example, "I would be singing if it were sunny", refers to the event of singing, conditional on the state that the weather is sunny.

"I would have been singing, had it been sunny", likewise refers to singing that would have happened at some stage in the past, conditioned on a the past event (in this case, again, the event being the existence of "sunny weather").

Conditionals are used in Shona much like they are in English. The rule for forming "would be" and "would have been", in Shona, is as follows:

Rule for Conditional "1" progressive (would be)

pronoun + "ngadai" + pronoun + "chi" + verb
eg. Ndi + "ngadai" + ndi + "chi + geza = ndi**ngadai** ndi**chi**geza
I would be washing

Rule for Conditional "2" progressive (would have been)

pronoun + "ngadai" + pronoun + "ka" + verb
eg. Ndi + **"ngadai"** + ndi **+ "ka" +** geza = ndi**ngadai** nd**aka**geza
I would have been washing

Some examples of the above two rules are shown below:
Ndingadai ndichibika dai[20] ndine[21] chikafu
I would cook if I had food

[20]"Dai" on its own with no pronoun means "if" or "if only".

[21]Note that for this sentence, in English, the action of cooking is predicated on the availability of food. In other words: The condition is that the food must first be available, after which, the action of "cooking" is then possible. Because the food is required first, it is talked about in the past compared to the action that depends on it, ie "I would be cooking if only I **had** food". In Shona the event on which the action is dependent on, can be referred to in the past or present, in effect meaning that it's quite correct to say (when translated literally) "I would be cooking if only I **have** food."

Ndingadai ndakabika dai ndine chikafu
I would have been cooking if only I had had food

Vangadai vachiseka dai vaenzi vari[22] pano
They would be laughing if the visitors were here

Vangadai vakaseka dai vaenzi vari pano
They would have been laughing had the visitors been here

Mungadai muchiona chii muTV?
What would you be watching on TV?

Mungadai makaona chii muTV?
What would you have been watching on TV?

Angadai achitaura nani paphone?
Who would he/she be speaking to on the phone?

Angadai akataura nani paphone?
Who would he/she have been speaking to on the phone?

Exercises

1. Convert the following into the *past progressive* tense
    a. Vari kushandira kuMutare
    b. Tiri kubikira chiremba chikafu
    c. Sadza ririkudyiwa neimbwa
    d. Tiri kumharwa nenhunzi
    e. Chitima chirikukwirwa nevanhu
    f. Movie irikufarirwa nevana
    g. Ndiri kutaurira sekuru nezve birthday rangu

[22] Note again that "vaenzi vari pano" translates literally to "the visitors are here", even though, in English, the correct translation is "the visitors were here".

2. Convert the following sentences to their past tense:
   a. Ndine chitoro pedyo neZvishavane
   b. Vana avo havana ruremekedzo nevakuru
   c. Ndine mari yakawandisa
   d. Hatina chikafu chose
   e. Mombe inenyanga huru
   f. Zvipikiri zvine ngura
   g. Handina mhanza

3. Convert the following from the form "was" to the form "used to" with one of the time phrases (gore rakapera, vhiki rakapera, mwedzi wakapera, nezuro, muna 2000, mwaka wechando wakapera, muna nyamavhuvhu, pakati peusiku, gore roga roga) and a location of your choice.
   a. Eg. Taibika tese
      Gore rakapera, taibika tese kumba kwaMai
   b. Nyati dzaidya uswa
   c. Mvura yainaya
   d. Mashizha aibhururutswa
   e. Vanababa vaigadzira pombi
   f. Jongwe raikukuridza
   g. Mbavha yaiba upfu
   h. Mapurisa aimisa midhudhudhu
   i. Amai vaitumira tsamba

4. Translate the following conditional tense sentences into English:
   a. Ndingadai ndichigadzira motokari dai ndine zvipanera
   b. Tingadai tichisimudza mapango dai tine tambo
   c. Tingadai tichihwanda mvura, dai tine tendi
   d. Vangadai vachishandira pamba dai vane wifi
   e. Huni dzingadai dzakagara dai tine magetsi
   f. Zvipatara zvingadai zvakavhura dai zvine mushonga
   g. Sadza ringadai rakadyiwa dai rine muriwo

Vocabulary

-bika	cook
-mhanya-mhanya	rush
-ona	see
-pfeka	wear
-takura	carry
-tamba	play
-taura	speak
bhururutswa	to be blown
gore rakapera	last year
gore roga roga	each and every year
hwanda	hide
kunze	outside
mhanza	luck
muenzi	visitor
muna nyamavhuvhu	in August
murwere	sick person
musoja	soldier
mvumo	permission
mwaka wechando wakapera	last winter
mwedzi wakapera	last month
ngura	rust
pakati peusiku	in the middle of the night
panguva iyoyo	at that time
muparidzi	priest
tambo	rope
tsva (adjective)	new
vhiki rakapera	last week
zororo	holidays

Lesson 4

ACTIVE AND PASSIVE VERBS

Active and passive verbs

In English, as in Shona, verbs are either "active" or "passive". An active verb communicates that something is performing an action and a passive verb communicates that something is having an action performed on it.

In the sentence, "the man cheats his boss", for example, the man is an actor who cheats his boss, so we consider the verb "cheat" to be active. In the sentence, "the boss was cheated by the man", the boss is being acted on, and because he is passive, the verb "cheat", is considered, likewise, to be in its "passive" form.

In English verbs are often made into their passive form by adding "ed" to them. There are, however, exceptions to this rule. "Drive", for example, becomes "driven" in the passive form and not "drived".

In Shona, as in English, there are active and passive forms of a verb. Fortunately, the rule for converting active to passive in Shona is consistent (unlike in English).

Rule: Converting verbs to their passive form
Verb minus last vowel + "wa"
eg geza minus "a" + "wa" = gezwa (washed)

Examples of active verbs and their passive counterparts are given below:

Active	**Passive**
tora take	torwa (taken) taken
peta fold	petwa folded
vaka build	vakwa built
ona see	onwa seen

punza break	punzwa broken
tema chop/hit	temwa chopped/hit
cheka cut	chekwa cut
nyora write	nyorwa written

Hare are some example sentences active and passive forms:

Active	**Passive**
mwana akatora beghi the child took the bag	beghi rakatorwa nemwana the bag was taken by the child
musevenzi akapeta gumbezi the worker folded the blanket	gumbezi rakapetwa nemusevenzi the blanket was folded by the worker
vavaki vakavaka madziro The builders built the walls	madziro akavakwa nevavaki the walls were built by the builders
vabereki vakaona gondo the parents saw the eagle	gondo rakaonwa nevabereki the eagle was seen by the parents
musikana akapunza hari the girl broke the clay pot	hari yakapunzwa nemusikana the clay pot was broken by the girl
mukomana akatema murume nedombo the boy struck the man with a rock	murume akatemwa nedombo nemukomana The man was struck by the rock of the boy
mubiki achacheka muriwo the cook will cut the vegetables	muriwo uchachekwa nemubiki the vegetables will be cut by the cook
mudzidzisi ari kunyora tsamba the teacher is writing the letter	tsamba iri kunyorwa nemudzidzisi the letter is being written by the teacher

Exercises

1. Convert the following passive sentences to their active form
    a. Eg. Miriwo iri kugezwa nemubiki
       Mubiki ari kugeza miriwo
    b. Gumbo rangu rakakuvadzwa nebhodhoro
    c. Ndiri kunetswa nemotokari yangu
    d. Sadza richapedziswa nemakonzo
    e. Mugwagwa wakagadziriswa nekanzuru
    f. Vakashandiswa naboss wavo
    g. Kitsi dzinodaidzwa naChipo
    h. Tichanyorerwa nezve madate ematesti nemudzidzisi wedu

2. Convert the following passage into its passive form, where possible.

   Mazuva ose chiremba vanoongorora murwere. Chiremba vanopa murwere mapiritsi. Masikati chiremba vanobaya jekiseni murwere uye manheru chiremba vanonyorera murwere prescription. Pashure chiremba vanotsanangurira murwere nezve kushandisa mapiritsi nguva dzose. Pashure, murwere anotenda chiremba.

Vocabulary

-cheka	cut
-chekwa	cut (passive)
-daidza	call
-kuvadzwa	injured by
-nyora	temwa
-nyorwa	chopped/hit
-ongorora	examine
-onwa	seen (passive)
-pedziswa	finished by
-peta	fold
-petwa	folded
-punza	break
-punzwa	broken (passive)
-tema	cut
-temwa	cut (passive)

-tenda	thank
-tora	taken
-torwa	taken
-tsanangura	explain
-vaka	build
-vakwa	built (passive)
dombo	rock
gondo	eagle
gumbezi	blanket
hari	clay pot
madziro	walls
musevenzi	worker
muvaki	builder
tsamba	letter

Lesson 5

VERB EXTENSIONS

Verb extensions

In lesson 4 we looked at how Shona verbs can be made into their passive form by removing the last syllable and adding "wa" at the end. This "wa" extension, in the case of making verbs "passive" is just one example of many ways in which verbs can be modified to change their meanings.

There is, unfortunately, no immediate parallel that can be drawn with the English language on the subject of these extensions. In English, word extensions are used, but they invariably convert adjectives into verbs and vice versa. For example, "legal" is an adjective in English, which can be modified to a verb with the extension "ise" to give "legalise", but there are no verbs that, with the addition of a suffix, change in meaning.

With Shona, in contrast, verbs are regularly modified with a series of suffixes in order to change meaning. For example, the word "gara" (to sit or remain) can be modified with the extension "ira" to give "garira" (to sit or remain **for** something or **at** some place). Similarly, the verb "mhanya" can be extended with "isa" to give "mhanyisa" (to run very fast).

The table, below, shows the two verb extensions that are commonly used in Shona, alongside their meanings.

Extension	**Meaning**
-ira (or –era)	specifies an action happening by someone or something, to someone or something or, depending on context, for the purpose of
-isa (or -esa)	emphasises abundance of something or, depending on context, refers to what person or object is performing what action on some other object/person

It might seem confusing at first glance that a single verb extension can mean two completely different things. Doing something for someone, for example, is very different to doing something at some place. How does a speaker avoid confusing one meaning with another? The reality is that the distinctions are obvious to a native speaker but not obvious at all to a second language speaker. Extensions are arguably the most difficult component of Shona and second language speakers must practice them to become familiar with their different uses.

A closer look at verb extensions is given below with many examples of the different contexts.

-ERA

We look here closely at how to distinguish between when someone is doing something to someone, or for someone, or for some purpose.

In short, the overall meaning of the verb with an extension depends to some extent on what the verb is, and on whether or not other verbs are involved in the sentence.

The different meanings are investigated with some examples. The sentence, "ndichatum**ira** chipo Tendai" translates to "I will send the gift **to** Tendai". In this case, the "era" extension shows who the gift is being given to. If we now include a verb in the sentence as follows, "ndichatum**ira** chipo Tendai kuwana mari", this translates to, "I will send a gift to Tendai **for the purpose of** getting money." Note that the addition of the verb changes the meaning from "to" to "for the purpose of".

If we look at a different verb, the "era" extension can mean something slightly different. For example, "mukadzi akapet**era** gumbezi mwana", translates to "the woman folds the blanket **for** the child". It would not make sense, in this case, to say, "the woman folds the blanket **to** the child". Note, therefore, that exactly what "era" means is very context dependent. If we were to once more add another verb to the sentence, we could, however, still change the meaning of "era" to mean, "for some purpose" or "in order to". For example, "mukadzi akapet**era** gumbezi mwana kurerutsa mutoro", translates to, "the woman folded the blanket for the child in order to reduce [its] workload"

verb	verb + extension	example
-peta to fold	-petera to fold (for [someone] or at [some place])	mukadzi akapet**era** gumbezi mwana the woman folded the blanket **for** the child

		mukadzi akapet**era** gumbezi kuisa mucupboard the woman folded the blanket **in order to** put it in the cupboard
-chera scoop/lift/fetch/ dig	-cherera to scoop lift for someobody or at [some place]	ndakacher**era** mvura sisi I collected water **for** my sister ndakacher**era** mvura kuchibhorani I collected water **at** the borehole ndakacher**era** mvura kugeza motokari I collected water **for the purpose of** cleaning the car
-gera shave	-gerera shave for some reason or at [some place]	takager**era** bvudzi kubhabha we cut our hair **at** the barber takager**era** bvudzi kupinda chiuto We cut our hair **for the purpose of** entering the army
-nyora -to write	-nyorera write for someone or at [some place]	vakanyor**era** tsamba Baba they wrote the letter **for** father vakanyor**era** tsamba kuchikoro they wrote the letter **at** school vakanyor**era** tsamba kutenda mudzidzisi They wrote the letter **in order to** thank the teacher

Below we now show the same verbs but with the addition of passive extension:

verb	verb + extension	example
-peta to fold	-peterwa to be folded (for [someone] or at [some place])	mwana akapet**erwa** gumbezi nemukadzi the child's blanket was folded [for him] by the woman gumbezi rakapet**erwa** kudziisa mwana The blanket was folded **in order to** warm the child
-chera scoop/lift/fetch/dig	-chererwa to scoop lift for someobody or at [some place]	ndakacher**erwa** mvura nasisi I had water collected for me by [my] sister ndakacher**erwa** mvura kuchibhorani water was collected for me from the borehole ndakacher**erwa** mvura kuchibhorani kunwa water was collected for me from the borehole in order to drink
-gera shave	-gererwa shave for some reason or at [some place]	takagererwa bvudzi kuchikoro our hair was cut at school takagererwa bvudzi kuenda kuchikoro our hair was cut **for the purpose of** going to school takagererwa bvudzi kubhabha naPeter our hair was cut **at** the barbour by Peter

-nyora -to write	-nyorera write for someone or at [some place]	Baba vakanyorerwa tsamba na Tatenda father's letter was written [for him] by Tatenda vakanyorerwa tsamba kuchikoro the letter was written [for them] at school tsamba yakanyorerwa baba naTatenda The letter was written by Tatenda to father tsamba yakanyorerwa baba kubvunza mari The letter was written to father in order to ask for money

-ISA

Below are some examples that should clarify how *–isa* is used. Where possible we use the same verbs as above in order to illustrate how the extension modifies verb meanings.

verb	**verb + extension**	**example**
-peta to fold	-petisa to fold (thoroughly/carefully, or with something)	petisa mbatya! fold the clothes carefully/thoroughly! petisa mbatya ne iyoni fold the clothes with the iron
-chera scoop/lift/fetch/ dig	-cherisa to scoop/lift vigorously or using [something]	cherisa mvura! Get water! [with emphasis on putting your back into it!]

		cherisa mvura nebucket get the water with the bucket
-gera shave	-geresa shave thoroughly or with [some implement]	geresa bvudzi! shave thoroughly geresa bvudzi rako nechigero cut your hair with the shaver
-nyora	-nyoresa write a lot or with some implement	ndichanyoresa vhiki rino bhuku I will write alot on my book this week ndichanyoresa bepanhau nechinyoriso I will write on the newspaper with a pen

Below we show the same verbs, now used with a combined passive extension

verb	verb + passive extension	example
-peta to fold	-petiswa to be folded (thoroughly/carefully, or by something)	mbatya dzinopetiswa na John The clothes are folded thoroughly by John mbatya dzinopetiswa neiyoni The clothes are folded with the iron
-chera scoop/lift/fetch/dig	-cheriswa to be scooped/lifted vigorously or using [something]	mvura yakacheriswa naShingi! a lot of water was collected by Shingi mvura yakacheriswa ne bucket the water was collected with the bucket
-gera shave	-gereswa shaved thoroughly	bvudzi riri kugereswa kutaundi

	by something [or with some implement]	the hair is being shaved in town bvudzi rako riri kugerewsa nechigero your hair is being shaved by the shaver
-nyora -to be tired	-nyoresa write a lot or with some implement	vhiki rino bhuku richanyoreswa neni this week the book will be written on a lot by me bepanhau richanyoreswa nechinyoriso the newspaper will be written on with a pen

Exercises

1. Extend the following verbs with *ira/era*:
    a. Eg. Fara
    b. Geza
    c. Bika
    d. Gara
    e. Simudza
    f. Punza
    g. Pwanya
    h. Dzvinya
    i. Potsa
2. Extend the verbs in question 1, above, with *isa*.
3. Translate the following sentences into English:
    a. Eg. Mazuva ose mukomana anotumira zvidhina kuvaka imba
    Every day the boy sends bricks [in order] to build the house
    b. Mazuva ose mukomana anotumira zvidhina John
    c. Vabereki vachanyorera tsamba vana
    d. Ndine mhanza nekubatsirwa kutora driver's license naJohn

e. Tinoda kutengerwa mapiritsi kuchitoro
f. Chimbuzi chirikugadzirwa kuzoshandiswa kumutambo
g. Mapango akavezerwa kuvaka chimufananidzo
h. Vaitaurira Shephard nezve mapurisa

4. Translate the following into English:
   a. Tiri kushandiswa nemabhengi kubvuma mabondi
      Eg. We are being used by the banks to accept bond notes
   b. Mhanyisa kundotengesa[23] fodya kuchitoro
   c. Sungisa mapango newaya
   d. Simudzisa lintel netambo
   e. Tangisa sendenzi nevara guru
   f. KuSouth Africa kune zvinhu zvaunoda zvakawandisa
   g. Musawanzisa shuga mucoffee yangu
   h. Madomasi ari kukurisa gore rino nemvura yakawandisa

Vocabulary

-bvuma	accept
-gera	shave
-kura	grow
-simudza	lift up
-sunga	tie
-tanga	start
-wanza	top up
bvudzi	hair
chigero	shaver
chimbuzi	toilet
chimufananidzo	statue
domasi	tomato
iyoni	iron
piritsi	pill
shuga	sugar

[23]Note that "ku ndo[verb]" in this sentence means "for the purpose of" and therefore conveys the same meaning as a verb extended with "ira". In this particular example, it would have been just as accurate to say, "mhanyisira kutengesa fodya kuchitoro".

tuma	send
vara guru	capital letter

Lesson 6

AUXILIARIES TO VERBS

Auxiliaries to verbs

We have already seen in Chapter 4 and 5 that Shona verbs can be modified by extensions that subtly (or drastically) change their meaning. In this chapter we discuss auxiliaries to verbs. Auxiliaries (as they are often called) are modifiers that go between the pronoun and the verb (rather than, as we have seen in previous chapters, at the end of the verb) to add extra meaning. For example, the auxiliary "mbo" is often used to communicate something that someone "once" did. "Ndaka**mbo**enda kuMutare" means "I **once** went to Mutare". "Ndaka**mbo**ona shiri iyo kuGonarezhou" means "I **once** saw that bird at Gonarezhou".

Other infixes exist to communicate different things, as shown in table below:

Auxiliary	**Meaning**
mbo	once, ever or never
to	already
zo	finally
ngo	simply
ndo	in order to
fumo	early in the morning
garo	always
wanzo	frequently/often

We below examine each auxiliary in detail:

"Mbo" – once, or ever, or never (depending on context)

The infix "mbo", as we have seen in the above example, means "once" but it can also mean other things, depending on the context in which it's used. When used as a question, for example, "mbo" best translates to "ever", but when used with a negated verb, translates to "never". The rule box below makes the various distinctions clearer:

Rule: "mbo" (once, ever, ocassionally, never)
pronoun + tense + infix + verb (once)
eg nda+ aka + **mbo** + enda = ndaka**mbo**enda (I once went)

pronoun + habitual tense + infix + verb (sometimes, ocassionally)[24]
eg ndi+ no + **mbo** + enda = ndino**mbo**enda (I sometimes go)

pronoun + tense + infix + verb + "here?" (ever)
eg wa+ aka + **mbo** + enda + "here?"= waka**mbo**enda here? (Did you ever go?)

"ha" + pronoun + tense + infix + verb (never)
eg "ha" + ndi + **mbo** + enda = handi**mbo**enda (I **never** go)

Note that "mbo" is only ever used in the past or habitual tense. It is never correct to use it in the future as you might do in English. For example, "ndichambotenga imba here?", would in theory translate to, "will I ever by a house?", but does not, in fact, make sense in Shona.

Here are some further examples of "mbo" in a variety of contexts:

Taka**mbo**rwa navanachiremba nezve mishonga yekupa vana
We **once** fought with the doctors about which medicine to give the children

Taka**mbo**rasika kuKadoma
We **once** got lost in Kadoma

Ano**mbo**dzidzisa mathematics kuchikoro
He/she **sometimes** teaches mathematics at the school

Ndino**mbo**shupika nekutaura Chishona
I **sometimes** find it difficult to speak Shona

[24]Note that what makes the meaning "sometimes" rather than "once" is the fact that the habitual tense is used. When the habitual is applied in this way it communicates "occasionally".

Vaka**mbo**kwira here pagomo apo?
Have they **ever** climbed that mountain?

Waka**mbo**puta fodya here?
Have you **ever** smoked tobacco?

Handi**mbo**mhanya kuchitoro
I **never** run to the store

Haambosekerera pedyo ne mapurisa
I never smile next to policemen

Handina ku**mbo**pomera muningina pamusoro pekuba mari
I **never** accused my little brother of stealing money

"to" – already or must (depending on context)

The auxiliary "to" means "already" when used with a verb in the past tense, but means "must" when used with a verb in the present tense. The rule for using "to" in both contexts is shown in the rule box below:

Rule: "to" (already/must)
pronoun + past tense + "to" + verb (already)
eg nda + aka + **"to"** + tenga = ndaka**to**tenga mbatya (I **already** bought clothes)

pronoun + present tense + "to" + verb (must)
eg u + no + "to" + rovera chipikiri pa wall = uno**to**rovera chipikiri pa wall (you **must** hit the nail into the wall)

Note that "to" is never used with a future tense.

The below examples clarify the above use of "to":

Vaka**to**dzosera maplier
They **already** returned the pliers

Ta**to**bvisa zvidinha pamudhuri
We **already** removed the bricks from the wall

Aka**to**dzvinya bhatani yekuvura ghedhi
He/she **already** pressed the button to open the gate

Ndino**to**shingirira kubudirira muhupenyu
I **must** persevere to succeed in life

Muno**to**shandisa wire kusunga ghedhi kumapole
You (plural) **must** use the wire to tie the poles to the gate

Tapiwa ano**to**pasa maexem ake
Tapiwa **must** pass his exams

"zo" – finally, at last or very

The auxiliary "zo" means "finally", or "at last", but it can also mean "very", depending on the context. The rule is discussed below and the subtleties that distinguish "finally" from "very" are discussed later.

Rule: "zo" (finally, at last, eventually, or very)
pronoun + past tense + "zo" + verb
eg nda+ aka + **"zo"** + bika = ndaka**zo**bika mazai (I finally cooked eggs)

When intending to communicate "finally", *zo* is used to announce a final event happening after a series of preceding and connected events. For example, "I bought some Sunlight liquid and then, finally, washed the dishes" would translate in Shona to "ndakatenga Sunlight liquid uye ndaka**zo**geza ndiro". The "zo" in this case not only communicates that something was "finally" done, but also implies a causal chain. In the above example, then, the first event (buying dishwashing liquid) is connected to (and indeed, required for) the second event of washing dishes[25].

[25]The idea of "connected" events described with "zo" might sound quite foreign. But keep in mind that in English the word "finally" is often used in much the same way. In the sentence, "I finally made it to town today", for example, the word "finally" refers to a previous time in which there were obstacles that prevented

When "zo" is used with stative adjectives it tends to add emphasis to those adjectives in addition to (or instead of) communicating the idea of *finality*. Recall from the first introductory book, "Learning Shona: Zero to Functional in Twelve Lessons" that stative adjectives are formed from verbs that are used in their past tense to describe the present. Some simple stative sentences are given below:

Shona	**English**
akanaka	he/she is good
ndakafara	I am happy
takaneta	we are tired
vakadzidza	you (plural) or learned
shiri dzakawanda	many birds
mukomana akapusa	a stupid boy
chibage chakakura	a big mealie
musikana akafupika	a short girl

Because the above sentences use stative adjectives, then, injecting the auxillary "zo" into them adds emphasis to the adjective rather than expressly communicating the notion of *finality*. For example "akafara" (he/she is happy) can be modified to "aka**zo**fara" (he/she is very happy). Likewise, "musikana akafupika" (the girl is short) can be modified to "musikana aka**zo**fupika" (the girl is very short).

The below examples clarify the use of "zo":

Nezuro takagadzirisa motokari. Nhasi ta**zo**enda kuNyanga
Yesterday we fixed the car. Today we **finally** went to Nyanga

Imbwa yakarwara svondo rakapera, pashure yaka**zo**fa
The dog was sick last week, and **eventually** died afterwards

Imbwa yakabata tsuro vhiki rakapera uye nyama yetsuro yaka**zo**biwa nembava

town being reached. The final act of reaching town, therefore, is connected to a bunch of inferred previous events. Likewise, in the sentence, "I studied hard and then finally passed the exam", the word "finally" connects the final act of passing the exam to the previous event of studying.

The dog caught the hare last month and its meat was [**eventually**[26]] stolen by thieves

Ndaka**zo**budirira kutora driver's license pashure pekutadza kutora makore matatu
I **finally** succeeded in getting a driver's license after failing to get it for 3 years

Maka**zo**tuma ani kuBotswana kutora passport yenyu
Who did you **finally** send to Botswana to collect your passport?

Nda**zo**neta
I am **very** tired

Ta**zo**tadza
We failed **badly**

Maka**zo**mira
You waited for a **long time**

Gudo ra**zo**pusa
The baboon is **very** stupid

Mbizi ya**zo**kura
The giraffe is **very** big

Poto yaka**zo**sviba
The pot is **very** dirty

---

[26]Note that in English the word "finally" isn't really needed to make the sentence sound correct. Keep in mind, however, that in Shona, "zo" is used far more commonly than "finally" would be in English. In fact, "zo" can be used at any time that you wish to emphasise that one event is connected to another.

"ngo" – "just" or "simply"

In English the word "just" has many meanings:

1. It can mean "only" or "simply". For example, "would you like another biscuit?" "Okay, but *just* one more".
2. It can be used to add emphasis to a statement. For example, "the dress is just too expensive".
3. It can reduce the force of a statement. For example, "I just want to borrow the car for one day."
4. It can mean "almost" or "almost not". For example, "we arrived at the station just in time to catch the train" and "we've just about finished decorating the room"
5. It can mean "very" or "completely". For example. "What she did is just insane"
6. It can mean "fair" or "morally correct." For example, "The sentence given to the thief was just."

Of the above meanings of "just", the Shona "ngo" maps best to point 1 ('only' or 'simply') and to point 3 (reducing the force of a statement).

The rule for using "ngo" is shown below:

Rule: "ngo" ("just" or "simply")
pronoun + tense + infix + verb
eg nda+ aka + **ngo** + enda = ndaka**ngo**enda kutaundi kutenga chingwa (I simply went to town to buy bread)

Below are some examples using "ngo":

Nda**ngo**svika nhasi kubva kuSouth Africa
I **just** arrived today from South Africa

Mvuu yaka**ngo**fa pasina yambiro
The hippopotamus **just** died without warning

Vakomana vaka**ngo**tadza kukwira bhazi
The boys **simply** failed to get on the bus

Ndicha**ngo**taura zvishoma pameeting
I will **just** talk a little at the meeting

Zvitima zvicha**ngo**fa zvisina kugadzirwa
The trains will **simply** break without being repaired

Ano**ngo**taura zvisina basa[27]
He/she just speaks nonsense

"ndo" – "in order to"

In English the phrase "in order to" connects one action with another. For example, "I went to town *in order* to watch the concert" connects the act of being in town with the purpose of watching a concert.

In Shona, the phrase "in order to" is conveyed with the auxiliary "ndo". The rule for applying this in sentences is shown below.

Rule: "ndo" ("in order to")
[sentence of action] ku + "ndo" + verb
eg [ndichauya] ku + "ndo" + batsira = ndichauya kundobatsira (I will come in order to help)
(note in the example above that the sentence of action (denoted in square brackets) refers to the first action on which the purpose of the second action is built)

The below examples make the use of "ndo" clearer:

Takafamba kwaBaba ku**ndo**tora chibage
We went to father's place **in order to** get maize

Vachapiwa petrol kun**do**zadza motokari
They will be given petrol **in order to** fill up the car

[27] "zvisina basa" literally means "without work", but translates best to "without meaning" or as "nonsense".

Shiri ichabhuruka ku**ndo**mhara pamuti
The bird will fly **in order to** land on the tree

Mapanga akarodzwa ku**ndo**cheka nyama
The knives were sharpened **in order to** cut the meat

Mapurisa vakamisa motokari ku**ndo**tora mari kubva kunadriver
The policemen stopped the car **in order to** get money from the driver

Vakatema mapango kun**do**vaka imba
They cut the poles **in order to** build the house

"Fumo" – "early in the morning"

In Shona the formal way of saying, "early morning" is, "mangwanani-ngwanani". One can, however, use the auxiliary "fumo" to mean the same thing.

Rule: "fumo" ("early in the morning")
pronoun + tense + "fumo" + verb
eg nda + aka + "**fumo**" + enda = ndaka**fumo**enda kuchitoro (I went to the store early in the morning)

The examples below make the use of the above rule clearer:

Ndicha**fumo**geza mangwana
I will wash **early in the morning** tomorrow

Sekuru vaka**fumo**dziya moto
Grandfather warmed himself by the fire **early in the morning**

Hanga yaka**fumo**chema
The guineafowl called **early in the morning**

Mvura yaka**fumo**naya nezuro
The rain fell **early in the morning** yesterday

Nda**fumo**dya chikafu kuma 5am[28]
I ate food **early this morning** at 5am

Ucha**fumo**chera mvura mangwana here?
Will you collect water **early** tomorrow **morning**?

Garo – always

In Shona, "garo" means "always". This translation is exact and not context dependent. Note that garo refers to an action that is habitual, and therefore must be used with a tense that is habitual, or future. For this reason, garo cannot be used with the recent or remote past.

Rule: "garo" ("always")
pronoun + tense + infix + verb
eg nda + ai + **garo** + enda = ndai**garo**enda kuchitoro (I always used to go to the store)

For example:

Ndicha**garo**gara pedyo newe
I will always remain by your side

Vano**garo**tukana kuchitoro
They **always** shout at each other at the store

Michero ino**garo**tengeswa naMai
The fruits are **always** sold by mother

Musoja ano**garo**rova mukadzi
The soldier **always** hits the woman

Ndai**garo**ziva chokwadi nezve nyaya iyoyo
I have **always** known the truth about that story

[28]Note that because the tense is recent past, that it already implicitly communicates that eating happened *today* and, therefore, there is no need to add "nhasi" to clarify that it happened today.

Nguva iyoyo, ndai**garo** ziva kuti muchauya
At that time, I was **always** aware that you would come

Chipatara chikuru chino**garo**shaya mishonga
A big hospital **always** runs out of medicine

Wanzo – frequently/often

"Wanzo" is etymologically derived from the verb "-wanza", which means "to increase". When modified to become the auxiliary "wanzo" it means "frequently" or "often". Since, like "garo", it refers to habitual actions it must, likewise, be used with the habitual (or future) tense.

Rule: "wanzo" ("frequently"/"often")
pronoun + tense + infix + verb
eg nda + aka + **wanzo** + enda = ndino**wanzo**enda kuchitoro (I frequently go to the store)

For example:

Ndino**wanzo**tadza kuverenga chindevere
I **often** struggle to read Ndebele

Vano**wanzo**tsvaira panze
They **often** sweep outside

Pakupedza kusevenza, ndino**wanzo**neta
After finishing work, I'm **often** tired

Nguva yechando tino**wanzo**rwara
In the winter season we're **often** sick

Nemapurisa kwese kwese mazuva ano, nyaya seidzi dzino**wanzo**konzeresa madambudziko
With police everywhere these days, stories like these **frequently** cause problems

Muno muZimbabwe mapato akasiyana siyana akawanda ano**wanzo**r-wisana
In Zimbabwe the many different political parties **frequently** fight one another

Exercises

1. Translate the following into Shona, using mbo, to, ndo, zo, fumo, wanzo, where necessary:
    a. eg. I have never gone to South Africa
       Handina ku**mbo**enda kuSouth Africa
    b. I once saw a leopard
    c. Have you already returned the scissors?
    d. He helped fix the car and then, finally, drove home
    e. I ran to the store early in the morning in order to buy milk, but saw that ther store was already closed
    f. In my heart of hearts I already know the truth
    g. At work I frequently embarrass[29] myself by arriving late
    h. The rat ate all the food but, after some days, it finally died of starvation
    i. They worked in order to save for a good holiday
    j. Have you ever seen a person with such a good heart?
    k. I thought that you had already found a job that you want

2. Translate the following passage into English:
   Gore roga roga ndaiwanzoenda kuzororo kuNyanga kupurazi kweshamwari yangu kundomubatsira nebasa. Panguva iyoyo ndaifumomuka kundochengetedza zvipfuyo. Ndaisevenza chaizvo kuzvitarisa, asi rimwe zuva imwe mbudzana yakatanga mhanya-mhanya kwese kwese. Ndakaedza

[29]Note that you will need to use a reflexive here!

kuidzora asi ndakatadza. Mbudzana yakazorasika. Handina ku-zombo[30]iona zvakare.

Vocabulary

-budirira	succeed
-dzora	shepherd [back somewhere]
-dzosera	return [something]
-dzvinya	press
-konzeresa	cause
-kwira	climb
-mhara	land
-misa	stop
-nyadzisa	embarress
-pomera	accuse
-puta	smoke
-rasika	get lost
-rodzwa	be sharpened
-rwisana	fight one another
-shingirira	persevere
-shupika	find difficult
-sunga	tie
-tadza	fail
-zadza	fill up
bato	political party
chindevere	Ndebele language
chitima	train
chokwadi	truth
dambudziko	problem
dziya	warm
fodya	tobacco
fumo (auxillary)	early in the morning
garo (auxillary)	always
gonzo	rat
hanga	guineafowl
hupenyu	life

[30]Note that "zo" and "mbo" placed together is usually taken to mean "never ever"

kuzorora	on holiday[31]
kwese kwese	everywhere
mbiro	warning
mbo (auxillary)	once, ever or never
mbudzana	young goat
mhanya mhanya	run about
moyo	heart
mudhuri	wall
mukatikati memwoyo wangu	in my heart of hearts
muningina	small brother
mvuu	hippopatamous
ndo (auxillary)	in order to
ngo (auxillary)	simply
nyama	meat
purazi	commercial farm
sekerera	smile
shanwari	friend
shiri	bird
siyana siyana	different
to (auxillary)	already
tukana	mutually shout at or scold
wanzo (auxillary)	frequently/often
zo (auxillary)	finally
zvipfuyo	livestock

[31]Note that "zororo" is a noun derived from the verb "-zorora" (rest). As with its English counterpart, "holiday", however, the Shona "zororo" can be combined with a locative to mean "on holiday".

Lesson 7

CONJUNCTIONS

Conjunctions

A conjunction is a word that joins two or more other words together. They're often used to make language flow better and to connect ideas and/or predicate one action on the occurrence of another. Common English conjunctions are *for, and, but, yet, as soon as, as much as, although, because, by the time, in order that, lest, once* and *only if* (though there are more).

Below are some useful Shona conjunctions

Conjunction	**English meaning**
ne/na[32]	and/by/with
ne ku	and [when referring to places] or via [some place]
nyango/kana hazvo/kanapo	although/even though/despite/inspite of
nekuti/pamusoro pe	because
nezve	about
saka	so
nekudaro	hence/therefore
panguva iyo	at that time
kana	if/or/when/even
asi	but
sezvo	since
sekuti	for example

Examples of the conjunctions above are given below in a variety of contexts.

Ne/na - and/by/with

Tichaenda kutaundi **na**Phillip
We will go to town **with** Phillip

[32]Remember that "na" refers to people, street names, months and years. And remember that "ne" refers **only** to objects.

Tendai **na**Chipo vakabatsirana
Tendai **and** Chipo helped one another

Baba **na**Mai vanoseka nezve mitemo yehurumende
Father **and** mother laugh about the government's policies

Chitoro chiri pakati paJason Moyo **na**Kwame Nkurumah
The store is between Jason Moyo **and** Kwame Nkurumah [streets]

April naMay dzakapera
April **and** May have passed [literally: "have finished"]

2007 **na**2008 akanga ari makore akashata panyaya dzehupfumi wenyika
2007 **and** 2008 were bad years from an economic standpoint

neku – *and* (referring to places) or by (referring to verbs)

When referring to places, "neku" means "and", but when used in the context of verbs means "by" in the sense of indicating the means by which something is achieved.

Mapurisa vakaenda kuGweru **neku**Bulawayo
The policemen went to Gweru and to Bulawayo

Vasevenzi vari kugadzira mapango **neku**asunga newaya
The workers are fixing the poles **by** tying them with wire

Tichadraiva kuVic Falls **neku**Gokwe
We will drive to Vic Falls and to Gokwe

Ndichaenda kubasa **neku**movie, pashure ndichadzokera kumba
I will go to work **and** to a movie, afterwards I'll return home

Nzou dzakamhanya kugomo **neku**rwizi
The elephants to the mountain **and** the river

Mukadzi akagadzira juzi **neku**sonera machira akasiyana siyana
The woman made the jersey **by** sewing together different fabrics

Nyango/kana haszvo/kanapo – Although/despite/in spite of

Ndichanyora maexemineshoni **nyango** ndisina kuverenga
I will write the exams **although** I didn't study

Nguruve yakadya mumunda **nyango** kwainaya
The pig ate in the fields **although** it was raining

Zvimwe zvirimwa zvinogona kukura **kana hazvo** kusina mvura zhinji
Some crops are able to grow **despite** being without much water

Ndichashanda mazuva ose **kana hazvo** ndakaneta chaizvo
I will work every day **in spite of** being very tired

Ndege dzakabhururuka **kanapo** dzisina sevisi
The planes flew **despite** being without a service

Sekuru vaenda kuUSA **kanapo** ambuya vakavarambidza
Grandfather went to the USA **despite** grandmother disallowing him

Nekuti/pamusoro pe – because

Note that "pamusoro pe[33]" can also mean "about", depending on its context. In the next section its use as "about" will be considered further.

Nhasi ndanetswa nemapurisa **pamusoro pe**license disk yangu yakaexpaya
Today I was hassled by the policemen because my license disk expired

[33]"Pamusoro pe" literally means "on the head of", which translates well to "because", but it can, as mentioned in previous chapters, also mean "about".

Ambuya vanoda kurara **nekuti** vakaneta
Grandmother wants to sleep **because** she's tired

Vakaita tsaona **nekuti** vakatadza kuona gomba
They had an accident **because** they failed to see the ditch

Ndinoda basa ritsva **nekuti** zvinhu zvakaoma
I need a new job **because** times are hard

Amai vakataura **pamusoro pe**utsanana
Mother talked **about** hygiene

Akabudirira **pamusoro pe**kusevenza chaizvo
He succeeded **because** of working hard

Nezv[e/a]/pamusoro pe – About/concerning

In English, the word "about" means "concerning" or, depending on the context, it can indicate movement within a particular area. "Nezve" in Shona, however, translates only to "about" in the sense of "concerning" and never refers to movement within some place or area.

Note that when using the word, "tsanangura" (explain), that it should always be used with "nezve", literally meaning, "explain how to".

Below are some examples of "nezve"/"pamusoro pe" and "tsanangura":

Nhasi tichapindura mibvunzo **nezve** dambudziko remvura
Today we will tackle questions **concerning** [our] water problems

Mudzidzisi akatsanangura **nezve** nhoroondo yeZimbabwe kuvadzidzi
The teacher explained Zimbabwean history to the students

Mekanika **akatsanangura**[34] **nezve** kubvisa vhiri pamotokari
The mechanic explained how to remove the wheel from the car

---

[34]"Kutsanangura" (to explain) is always used with "nezve", much like "explain" is almost always used with "how to". Indeed, "tsanangura nezve" translates perfectly to "explain how to".

Ndichanyora bhuku **pamusoro pe**kudzidza chiShona
I will write a book **about** learning Shona

Mutungamiriri webato achagadzira mitemo **nezve** immigration
The leader of the party will make laws **concerning** immigration

Makambonzwa **nezva**[35] Brett Muvheti?
Have you ever heard **about** Brett Muvheti?

Zvinogoneka here kutaura **nezve** hupfumi wenyika mazuva ano, zvisina kutya?
Is it possible to talk **about** economics these days, without fear?

Saka – so

Ndiri kudzidza biology **saka** rimwe zuva ndichava chiremba
I am learning biology **so** that some day I can be a doctor

Saka[36], ndichaita sei mangwana kana mvura yapera?
So, what will I do tomorrow when the water runs out?

Mhara yakatsvedza **saka** yakadyiwa nembada
The impala slipped, **so** it was eaten by the leopard

Hakuna security ikoko, **saka** mbava dzinogona kupinda
There is no security over there, **so** thieves will be able to enter

Vari kukakavadzana **saka** havachawana nzira yekubatsirana
They are arguing with each other **so** they won't find a way to help each other

[35]Note that when talking about a person "nezva" is used instead of "nezve". This distinction is similar to that discussed for "na" and "ne" regarding people and objects, respectively.
[36]It is quite common for Shona speakers to begin sentences with "saka". Also, keep in mind that when a question begins with "saka" there is no need to add the usual component "ko" (tell me) to the sentence at either the beginning or the end.

Mishonga yakapera kuzvipatara, **saka** vanachiremba havagoni kubatsira vanhu
The medicine has run out at the hospitals, **so** the doctors aren't able to help people

Nekudaro – Hence/and therefore

Takatendekana **nekudaro** hatichavane HIV
We are faithful to each other **and therefore** we won't get HIV

Hapana munhu ane mari **nekudaro** maprice arikudzika
Nobody has money **and therefore** prices are dropping

Ndinosevenza chaizvo **nekudaro** ndichavane mari yakawanda yekuenda kuzororo
I work hard **and therefore** I will get a lot of money to go on holiday

Dzimwe nguva anoba zvimwe zvinhu **nekudaro** anogona kusungwa rimwe zuva
Sometimes he steals things **and**, **therefore**, might be arrested some day

Pakusvika pano akarasa phone yake **nekudaro** haugoni kutaura naye
On arriving here he lost his phone **and therefore** you won't be able to talk to him/her

Mombe dzose dzakatiza kubva mafuro **nekudaro** handigoni kudziendesa kuabattoir
All the cows fled the field and **therefore** I'm unable to send them to the abattoir

Panguva iyo – At that time

This phrase is useful when talking about a particular period in history. Note, also, that you can add extra emphasis to the particular time by placing an extra "yo" suffix at the end of "iyo" to give the phrase "panguva iyo**yo**", meaning "at that **particular** time".

Panguva iyo ndaidzidzisa kuScotland
At that time I used to teach in Scotland

Panguva iyo hapana aiziva kuti ndiani[37] achawina
At that time nobody knew who would win

Panguva iyoyo varume vashoma vaigona kugadzira motokari
At that particular time there were few men who were able to fix a car

Panguva iyo kune zvinhu zvijhinji muzvitoro
At that time there were many things in the stores

Panguva iyoyo ndaiva jaya
At that particular time I was a young man

Panguva iyo zvaigoneka kutengesa mombe
At that time it was possible to sell cattle

Kana – If /when/or/even

You will already have seen "kana" being used as "if" in the first book, "Zero to Functional in 12 Lessons". "Kana" does, however, have other meanings, depending on the context it's used in, such as "or", "when" and "even".

KANA (AS "IF" OR "WHEN")

In English the word "if" can be used with verbs that are in their past or present form, but not with verbs that are in their future form. For example, in the sentence, "**If I find** the time, I will come" uses "if" with the verb "find" using the present habitual tense. Note that it does not make sense in English to say, "if I will find the time, then I will come".

[37] "kuti ndiani achawina" literally translates to, "that who will win". In Shona this is a common way of saying things like "I don't know who is able to" (handizivi kuti ndiani anogona kuita)."

In Shona, the word "kana", like its equivalent in English, is governed by the same tense rules. As with English, therefore, "kana" cannot be used with verbs conjugated in their future tense[38].

Note that In English, as in Shona, "if" and "when" often mean the same thing. For example, "I will buy a car **when** I win the lottery" means something very similar to "I will buy a car **if** I win the lottery". In Shona, if and when are likewise interchangeable[39], as the following examples show:

Kana ndichiwana nguva, ndichauya
If I find the time, I will come

Kana madya sadza, muchaita chii?
When you've eaten the sadza, what will you do?

Tichageza **kana** tawana sipho
We will wash **when** we have found the soap

Kana tichiwhina game iyi, tichaenda pamusoro petable
If we win[40] this game, we will go to the top of the table

Kana ndawana mari, ndichazorora
When I have found money, I will rest

Kana mbada ichidya rimwe gudo, makudo ese achatya
If a leopard eats one baboon, all the baboons will become scared

Banga rinocheka **kana** rakapinza
The knife cuts **if** its sharp

---

[38]If you want to say "if" in Shona, but refer to something in the past that did not happen, like, for example, "If only I had known", you must use the Shona, "dai", meaning "if only".
[39]Note that another way of saying "when" is with "pa". This alternative is discussed in the chapter, "Miscellaneous language need-to-knows".
[40]When translating to English the closest correct way of saying this is "we win".

Kana (as "or")

In English, a sentence never begins with the word "or". Shona is the same. Therefore, it should be obvious that when a sentence begins with "kana" that it means "if" or "when" and not "or". When "kana" is used to mean "or", it always separates two nouns, or two actions.

Munofanira kutenga nhanga **kana** mbambaira
You must buy pumpkin **or** sweet potatoes

Unza passport yako **kana** national ID kana driver's license
Bring your passport, **or** national ID, or driver's license

Ndinokumbirawo nhondo yemiti **kana** nhondo yemaruva, chero achikura zvakanaka
I would like seedlings of trees, **or** seedlings of flowers, so long as they grow well

Changamire, munoda nyama yehuku here, **kana** yemombe?
Sir, would you like chicken **or** beef?

Mbudzi dzichaenda kunourayiwa nhasi **kana** mangwana here?
Are the goats going to be slaughtered today **or** tomorrow?

Motokari iri kushanda **kana** yakafa here?
Is the car working **or** is it dead?

Kana (as "even" or "even if")

In English, the word "even" can:

1. Describe something flat and smooth (for example, "the surface of the table is even")
2. Mean equal in number or value (for example, "an even gender balance among staff and children")
3. Mean divisible by two without a remainder (as in 2, 4, 6, 8, 10...)

4. Emphasise something surprising or extreme (for example, "even the brightest of the children failed the test")

In Shona, "kana" is used only as definition, 4, above. Distinguishing "kana", in the context of "even" or "even if" from "if", "when" and "or" depends entirely on the context of its use. The below examples should make the above rules clearer:

Kana vatungamiriri vakanaka, vane huori[41]
Even good leaders are corrupt

Kana Husein Bolt akakundikana kuwana mubairo
Even Husein Bolt failed to get a medal

Ndichaedza kuenda kuNyanga **kana hazvo**[42] handina petrol yakakwana
I will try to go to Nyanga **even though** I don't have enough petrol

Kana Pick'n Pay haina mukaka
Even Pick'n Pay doesn't have milk

Note that when using "kana" to mean "even if", the verb immediately following must always be conjugated in the recent past tense, despite the fact that it translates best to being a present tense in English. For example:

Kana mudhudhudhu wagadzirwa, haumbosviki kuMarondera
Even if the motorbike is fixed, it will never reach Marondera

Kana ndaenda kubhengi ndichashaya mari
Even if I go to the bank, I will fail to find money

Kana tabika chikafu ichi, hatigoni kugutsa vose
Even if we cook this food, we will be unable to feed them

---

[41]"huro" is used as a noun "to have corruption" and is therefore conjugated with the verb "to have" rather than the verb "to be".
[42]Note that "kana hazvo" means "even though" or "although" and was covered previously on page 78.

Asi – But

Ndichaenda kutaundi **asi** handichatenga chikafu
I will go to town **but** I won't buy food

Imba yakashata **asi** inodhurawo
The house is ugly **but** it is also expensive

Vanhu vese vari kuratidzira **asi** havagoni kuchinja chinhu
The people are protesting **but** they are unable to change anything

Mombe dzese dziri kurwara **asi** dzichatengeswa nemari yakawanda
All the cows are sick **but** they will still be sold for a lot of money

Ndine gumbo asi ndichamhanya mangwana
I have a [sore] leg but I will still run tomorrow

Anoda kutaura asi anokakama
He/she wants to speak but has a stutter

Sezvo – since

In English the word "since" has two meanings:

1. In the intervening period between (the time mentioned) and another time under consideration. For example, "she has been empathetic since she was sixteen".

2. "For the reason that" or "because". For example, "conservationists were delighted, since better protection of habitats would support higher wild dog populations".

In Shona, "sezvo" refers to the second meaning.

For example:

Tichashaya mari **sezvo** kune crash-crisis
We will fail to find money **since** there's a cash crisis

Michero yakaora **sezvo** magetsi akaenda
The fruit went bad **since** the power went out

Hapana anoziva kuti petrol yachauya rini, **sezvo** nyika haina mari
Nobody knows when the petrol is coming, **since** the country has no money

Vacheche havachemi **sezvo** vakaguta
The babies aren't crying **because** they're full

Vanyori vari kunyora **sezvo** kune nyaya dzinonakidza mazuva ano
The writers are writing **since** there are interesting stories these days

Sezvo takabatana tinogona kukunda
Since we work together, we are able to win

Sekuti – For example/such as

In Shona, "sekuti" is used exactly in the same way as "for example" is used in English. Keep in mind, however, that if you conjugate "ita" for some noun class and place it before "sekuti", it changes the meaning from "for example" to "like" or "such as".

For example, "takadya chikafu **chakaita sekuti** mazai nestrawberries" translates to "we ate food **such as** maize and strawberries".

The examples below should clarify the above explanation:

Takabhadara miripo nezve mhoszva dzakawanda, **sekuti** kushaya fire extinguisher, kushaya spare-wheel neover-speeding.
We paid many fines, **for example**, for failing to have a fire extinguisher, for failing to have a spare wheel, and for over-speeding.

Vakadzidza zvinhu zvakawanda kuchikoro, **sekuti** mathematics, physics neGeography
They learned a lot of things at school**, for example**, mathematics, physics and Geography.

Kune mhou dzakawandisa kuGonarezhou, **sekuti** mhara, chipembere uye twiza
There are many animals at Gonarezhou, **for example**, impala, rhino and giraffe.

Mutambo wenhabvu waiva ne vanhu vane mukurumbira, **sekuti** David Beckham, Ronaldo, George Shaya we Zimbabwe.
The soccer game featured famous people, **for example,** David Beckham, Ronaldo and George Shaya of Zimbabwe.

Paweekend yoga yoga tinodya chikafu **chakaita sekuti** mazai, beconi uye pizza
Each and every weekend we eat food like eggs, bacon and pizza

KuAmerica ndakasangana nevanhu vane mukurumbira **vakaita sekuti** Larry Page, Beyonce uye Will Smith
In America I met with famous people **such as** Larry Page, Beyonce and Will Smith

Laven Bird gardens ine shiri dzakawanda dzakasiyana siyana **dzakaita sekuti** gondo, njiva uye zizi
Laven Bird gardens has many different birds, **such as** eagles, doves and owls

Exercises

1. For the following sentences, choose whether to use "ne", "na" or "neku".
    a. Eg. Taienda **na**Tendai kundochera mvura
       We used to go **with** Tendai to collect water
    b. Hapana anoziva kuti Jim ___shamwari yake vaenda kupi
    c. Chipembere chichanwa mvura ___dzimwe mhou kurwizi
    d. Pazororo tichafamba kuTriangle ___Chimanimani
    e. Vakaendeswa _chiremba kuchipatara ___pharmacy
    f. Pakusvika kuNgomakurira ___Domboshava, Trevor ___Farai vakadzinga makudo ___tsoko
    g. Tichavhara maburi ___isa putty mukati
    h. Nyoka dzakapinda mumba ___kwira madziro

2. Translate the following into Shona, paying attention to the use of "nokuti" and "pamusoro pe" when translating "because", "on account of", or "through".
    a. I succeeded at the exam **because** I studied
       Eg. Ndakabudirira bvunzo **nokuti** ndakaverenga
    b. Everyone knows the truth **because** they speak to experts
    c. The plane crashed **because** the engines failed
    d. The economy failed **because** of bond notes
    e. The dogs survived the winter **on account of** finding food
    f. The policeman found the thief **through** examining some foot-prints
    g. Motocars can break down **on account of** poor maintenance
    h. They are going on holiday **because** they found enough money

3. Translate the following passage into English (with special emphasis on thinking about "sezvo", "kana", "kana hazvo", "asi" and "nyango"):

   Pandaisevenza kuGokwe ndaiziva mumwe mukadzi aiva nemwoyo wakanaka **nyango** aiva nehupenyu hwakaoma. **Sekuti**, rimwe zuva nda-kaona mukadzi uyu akabatsira mukomana akanga asina chinhu chose. **Panguva iyoyo** ndaiona kuti vanhu vese vakanga vari mumatambudziko ikoko kuGokwe. Nguva dzose ndaishamisika kuti sei mukadzi uyu aiva nemwoyo wakachena. Takapesana **sezvo** ndaifanira kudzoka kuHarare **kana hazvo** ndaida kugara ikoko.

4. Translate the following into Shona (with special emphasis on using "hence" or "therefore"):
    a. Eg. The workers help each other and, hence, the business works well
       Vasevenzi vanobatsirana nekudaro basa rinofamba zvakanaka
    b. The teachers know how to teach, therefore, their students know a lot
    c. The car hit the pothole and, henceforth, crashed into the lorry
    d. Hungry leopards look for food on farms and, as such, kill many goats
    e. The journalist will ask probing questions and, henceforth, get into trouble
    f. When repairing the car, you will see where the hole is and, therefore, know where to put the putty
    g. Those particular doctors have no medicines and, as such, are unable to help their patients
    h. The bond notes have entered the market and, as such, have caused inflation

Vocabulary

-batana	work with each other
-bhururuka	fly
-chema	cry
-draiva	drive
-expaya	expire
-gutsa	feed
-kakama	stutter
-kakavadzana	argue with one another
-nakidza	interest
-pindura mibvunzo	tackle questions
-rambidza	disallow
-rayiwa	get slaughtered

-shamisika	surprise/shock
-shata	bad/rotten/ugly
-sonera	sew
-tendekana	faithful
-tiza	flee
-tya	afraid
-wina	win
asi	but
changamire	sir
chero	so long/since
chipembere	rhino
dhura	expensive
gumbo	leg
huori	corruption
jaya	young man
kana	if/or/when/even
maruva	flowers
mbambaira	sweet potatoes
mhara	impala
mhosva	a wrong/crime
mubairo	medal
mucheche	baby
mukurumbira	fame
muripo	fine (cash)
mutambo	game
mutemo	law
mutungamiriri	leader
ndege	aeroplane
ne ku	and [when referring to places] or via [some place]
ne/na	and/by/with
nekudaro	hence/therefore
nekuti/pamusoro pe	because
nezve	about
nhabvu	soccer
nhanga	pumpkin
nhondo	seedlings
nhoroondo	history
nyango	although/even though
nyika	land
nzou	elephant

panguva iyo	at that time
saka	so
sekuti	for example
sevisi	service
sezvo	since
sipho	soap
tsaona	accident
twiza	giraffe
utsanana	hygiene
vhiri	wheel
waya	wire
zhinji	a lot
zvinogoneka	it is possible

Lesson 8

MISCELLANEOUS

Miscellaneous

In this chapter we discuss a number of miscellaneous (but arguably crucial) Shona language components. Many of these are subtle aspects of the language, but are nevertheless necessary to master the language.

Reciprocals

A reciprocal is a pronoun or verb expressing mutual actions or relationships. In English, examples of this include, "the boys fought each other", "we brushed each other's teeth", "we debated each other". In Shona, reciprocals are generated by adding a "na" at the end of a verb as the rule box, below, demonstrates:

Rule: Reciprocals

pronoun + tense + verb + "na"
eg. taka + ona + "na" = takaona**na** (we saw **each other**)

Common verbs to which reciprocals are applied include:

Shona	**English**
ona	see
onana	see each other
funga	think/miss
fungana	miss each other
tuma	send
tumana	send each other
geza	wash
gezana	wash each other
tuka	scold
tukana	scold each other
kudza	to respect
kudzana	to respect each other

dzidzisa	teach
dzidzisana	teach each other
rova	hit
rovana	hit each other
seka	laugh
sekana	laugh at each other
batsira	help
batsirana	help each other
takura	carry
takurana	carry each other
mhoresa	greet
mhoresana	greet each other
pfura	shoot/pass
pfurana	shoot/pass each other
dhuma	bump
dhumana	bump into each other
tengesa	sell
tengesana	sell each other [out]
pa	give
panana	give each other
netsa	bother
netsana	bother each other

Below are some examples of reciprocals in use:

Musikana wangu neni tinokudzana
My girlfriend and I respect each other

Pakugara kuScotland taimbomhoresana
When living in Scotland we used to sometimes greet each other

Motokari dzedu dzakadhumana mwedzi wakapera uye dzakaparara
Our cars crashed into each other last month and were written off

Maminister vakatengesana nezve nyaya yestayaway munaJuly 2016
The ministers sold each other out over the stayaway of July 2016

Mapurisa nevatyairi vemakombi vanonetsana
The police and the kombi drivers irritate each another

Musoja nembavha vakapfurana pashure pekuitirana[43] nharo
The soldier and the thief shot each other after an argument

Reflexives

A reflexive verb is a verb in which the object is the same as its subject. For example, "he washes himself" refers to someone, "he" (the subject) performing an action on "himself" (the object).

Some further examples in English include:

I brush my teeth

She drives herself

They don't behave themselves

We like ourselves

[43]In Shona "pekuitirana nharo" literally means "to do each other an argument", but translates to "have an argument with each other."

In Shona a reflexive is formed as shown in the rule box below:

Rule: Reflexives
pronoun + tense + "**zvi**"[44] + verb + pacha **+ possessive stem**
eg. ndino**zvi**geza pacha**ngu** mazuva ose = I wash myself every day

For example:

Vano**zvi**dzidzisa pacha**vo** mathematics
They teach themselves mathematics

Tino**zvi**pfekedza pach**edu** tisati taenda kuchikoro
We dress **ourselves** before going to school

Mucha**zvi**sunga pachenyu pashure pekuziva chokwadi
You will hang yourself after knowing the truth

Waka**zvi**tambisira nguva pachako nekutsvaga mari ku South Africa
You wasted your time trying to earn money in South Africa

Ndiri ku**zvi**tambudza pacha**ngu** nezve rudo
I am troubling **myself** over love

Keep in mind that "zvi" when used in its reflexive form refers to some person (or some object) performing an action on themself (or itself). If the action does not reference the person (or object) directly, then "zvi" should be omitted. "He cuts the vegetables himself", for example, refers to a person that is performing an action on some vegetables rather than himself and, therefore, in Shona this translates to "anocheka muriwo pachake" and **not** "ano**zvi**cheka muriwo pachake".

[44]Note that using "zvi" just after the tense and before the verb, as demonstrated here, could also be used to refer to "things", "ndino **zvi**geza" thereby translating to "I wash the things". Note, however, that the existence here of "pacha" and the ensuing possessive stem is what makes the sentence reflexive. In short, whenever you see "zvi", together with "pacha", know that it is referring to a reflexive and not to some objects.

Note the difference of the below examples from the above ones:

Vari kuveza mapango **pachavo**
They are sanding the planks **themselves**

Takaenda kuNyanga **pachedu**
We went to Nyanga by **ourselves**

Huku dzichadya mbeu **pachadzo**
The chickens will eat the grain by **themselves**

Chikafu hachichaora **pachacho**
The food won't go off by **itself**

Imbwa ichapina mudhibhi **pachayo**
The dog will go into the [verterinary] dip **itself**

Ramba – to refuse/persist

In English there are those rare words that have very different meanings depending on their contextual use. A good example of this is the word "sanction". In the sentence, "he sanctions the use of violence", the verb sanction refers to "permitting" some action (in this case, violence). But in the sentence, "illegal immigrants should be sent home, their employers sanctioned and border controls strengthened", the verb "sanction" in this context means "punishment".

Shona exhibits the same inversion phenomenon. The verb "ramba", for example, can mean "to refuse" as in, for example, "anoramba kuenda kuchikoro" (he refuses to go to school). But it can also mean "to persist", as in the sentence "anoramba achienda kuchikoro" (he persists in going to school).

Rule: Ramba (refuse/persist)
Refuse: pronoun + tense + "**ramba**" + infinitve + verb
eg. tino**ramba** kutaura nemapurisa = we refuse to talk to the police

Persevere: pronoun + tense + "**ramba**" + pronoun + "**chi**" + verb
eg. Vakaramba vachiputsa dzimba = They persisted in destroying the houses

Examples of "the refuse" form:

Imbwa yaramba kudya mazai
The dog refused to eat the eggs

Machine inoramba kushanda necard
The machine refuses to work with the card

Hapana vanhu vacharamba kuvhota
Nobody will refuse to vote

Pakusvika pano mombe dzese dzicharamba kubuda mulorry
On arriving here the cattle will refuse to get out the lorry

Mapanga ese akaramba kucheka nyama
All the knives refused (ie were unable) to cut the meat

Gonhi riri kuramba kuvhura
The door is refusing to open

Examples of the "persevere" form:

Rambai muchienda kusvikira munaSamora Machel
Persevere [travelling] until you reach Samora Machel [road/avenue]

Ndinoda kuramba ndichiverenga mabhuku a Charles Mungoshi
I want to persevere in lessonreading Charles Mongoshi's books

Vakaramba vachimhanya sezvo vaitiza mapurisa
They persevered in running because they were fleeing the police

Acharamba achinyora bhuku rekutsanangura nezve hupfumi
He will persevere in writing a book that explains economics

Sipho akaramba achidraiva kuMasvingo kana hazvo vhiri remotokari in-eponji
Sipho persevered in driving to Masvingo despite the car tyre having a puncture

Sekuru naAmbuya vanoramba vachidya nyama kana hazvo havasina mazino
Grandfather and grandmother persevered in eating meat although they don't have teeth

Making comparisons with kupfura/pane

Comparing one thing with another is a common practice in Languages. In English such comparisons are often done with "more than/less than" and "better than/worse than". For example, "this cup has got more water in it than that one". "This person is less capable than that one."

The two main words for performing comparisons in Shona are "kupfura" (which means "more than") and "pane" (which means "than").

1. Kupfura

This exclusively means [this is] "more than" [that].

Rule: kupfura ("more than" or "exceeding")
when describing a verb:
pronoun + noun + "kupfura" + noun
eg. Tendai ane mari **kupfura** George = Tendai has **more** money **than** George [has]

2. Pane

Because "pane" translates to "than" in English, it must always refer to some quantity or quality under comparison.

Rule: Pane ("than")
when describing a verb:
pronoun + noun + adjective + "pane" + noun
eg. Tendai ane mari yakawandisa[45] **pane** yaGeorge = Tendai has **more** money **than** George has

The following examples illustrate the above rules:

Mukomana uyu mukuru **pane** uyo
This boy is bigger than that one

Musikana uyu wakanaka **pane** musikana uyo
This girl is nicer **than** that girl

Mayusa akanaka **kupfura** bond coins
US dollars are better **than** bond coins

Sadza rakanaka **kupfura** chingwa
Sadza is better **than** bread

Ndinoziva zvakawanda **kupfura** John nezve mitemo yehurumende
I know more **than** John about the government's policies

Pane[46] zvidinha zvakawanda **pane** uko
There are more bricks here **than** over there

[45]Note that in this case (compared to the above case involving "kupfura") that the adjective "yakawandisa" is used to qualify what "pane" is referring to. In the previous rule, "kupfura" already means "more than" so there is no need to include "yakawandisa" to indicate "more".
[46]Note in this sentence that "pane" is used in both contexts here. The first occurrence refers to "there is" or "there are" and the second occurrence refers to "than".

Muhoro wangu mutsva wakanaka **kupfura** wekare
My new salary is better **than** the old [one]

Anomhanya **kupfura** shamwari yake
He runs **faster** than his friend

Positive and negative imperatives

The imperative refers to commands or requests (including giving or denying permission for activities). There is nothing that explicitly makes a sentence imperative in English, except that the verb being used is directed at the second person by implication. A sign that says "Don't litter" is an order to you (the second person) not to litter. Likewise, "Use the sidewalk" is an order for you (once more, in the "second person") to use the sidewalk.

Imperatives in English can be softened by adding "Please" or "do". For example, "Please don't litter", or "Please use the sidewalk", changes an order into a request.

In Shona, imperatives are formed much as they are in English and refer, similarly, to the second person, "you", being ordered (or requested) to do something. If a Shona verb is only one syllable, note that an "i" must be placed at the beginning of the verb.

The following examples illustrate the above idea:

Shandisa sidewalk
Use the sidewalk

Uya kubasa nenguva
Come to work on time

Bvisa magrovo ako
Remove your gloves

Idya[47] chikafu chako
Eat your food

The order can be made more polite by adding "i" to the end of the verb being used. For example:

Shandisai sidewalk
Please use the sidewalk

Uyai kubasa nenguva
Please come to work on time

Bvisai magrovo enyu[48]
Please remove your gloves

Idyai chikafu chenyu
Please eat your food

To make an imperative negative put "sa" or "rega" in front of the verb, as the rule box demonstrates.

Rule: negative imperatives
1. "sa"
pronoun + "sa" + verb
eg. mu + "sa" + rasa marara = mu**sa**rasa marara (don't throw rubbish)

2. "rega"
"rega" + infinitive verb
eg. "rega" + kupinda mvura = rega kupinda mvura (don't enter the water)

Both "sa" and "rega" can be used interchangeably with one another, as the below examples illustrate:

---

[47]Note that "i" was added to the beginning of "dya" because "dya" (eat) is a single syllable.
[48]Note that "ako" was changed to "enyu" in this case to be consistent with the idea that respect and courtesy is being shown. Recall that "enyu" refers to "you" (plural) but also confers respect, much as it would in French or German.

Mwana, u**sa**nyora madziro
Child, don't write on the wall

Mu**sa**rima paduzi nerwizi
Don't cultivate close to the river

Regai kudraivha makadhakwa
Don't drive while you're drunk

Regai kumhanya nemotokari
Don't run with your car (ie. don't speed with your car)

Mu**sa**pe mukaka wemombe vacheche
Please don't feed cow's milk to babies

Rega kunwa mapiritsi aya nehwahwa
Don't take the pills with alcohol

U**sa**ita ruzha
Don't make noise

Regai kunetsa mhuka
Please don't bother the animals

Note, above, that adding an "mu" to "sa" and appending an "i" to "rega" convert the imperative to a more polite version, equivalent to a "please" in English.

Kunge/se (as though/like)

In English people often use similes to strengthen descriptions. "She is as stubborn as a mule", "he talks like a demagogue", "she thinks like a surgeon" are all examples of sentences making use of similes. In Shona, similes are formed using the word "kunge", which means "like" or "as though".

Anotaura **kunge** anoziva
He talks **as though** he is knowledgeable

Anehasha **se**shumba
She is angry **as** a lion

Vanoimba **kunge** vakawina makwikwi
They sing **as though** they have won the tournament

Kana taona mbava tichatiza **kunge** vanhu varikutyira hupenyu hwedu
We will run **as though** we are [people] freightened for our lives

Munofunga **kunge** muscientist
You think **like a** scientist

Munofunga **se**muscientist
You think **like a** scientist

Munotaura **kunge** muri muscientist
You talk **as though** you are a scientist

Ndinonyora **sa**Baba
I write **like** father

Ndaishingurira kusevenza **se**dhongi
I used to persevere **like** a donkey

Like this, like that

When demonstrating actions to other people we often make use, in English, of "like this" or "like that". On cooking shows, for example, the cook may say, "sauté the mushrooms like this", while demonstrating, visually, how to do it. When working in practical situations, like in building, or in agriculture, people are frequently called upon to demonstrate things to colleagues, and using "like this" and "like that" can, in those situations, be very useful.

"se izvi" means "like this" and "se izvo" means "like that", as shown in the following examples:

Rova mazai **se izvi**
Beat the eggs **like this**

Kurungai Sadza **se iszvi**
Stir the sadza **like this**

Enzanisa mapango ne spirit-level **se izvi**
Level the planks with the spirit level **like this**

Sanganisai simendi neivhu **se izvi**
Mix the cement and soil **like this**

Ndakagadzira motokari nemaplier **se izvo**
I fixed the car with the **pliers like that**

Taibika macake **se izvo**
We used to cook the cake **like that**

Vaisekesana **se izvo**
They used to make each other laugh **like that**

Chera gomba nebadza **se izvo**
Dig the hole with the badza **like that**

Nde [re/ye/dze/e/we/che/zve] [kuti] – is for/is about...

"Nde" on its own means "is for". It can be considered a particular conjugation of the verb "to be".

For example the sentence, "mari **nde ye**chikoro", translates to "the money **is for** school" where nde refers to "is" and "ye" refers to "for", conjugated for the soft sounding noun, "mari".

When used with a verb, it translates best to "for the purpose of".

The above rules are summarized in the box, below:

Rule: nde [re/ye/dze/e/we/che/zve]
1. "is for":
"nde" + noun conjugation[re/ye/dze/e/we/che/zve] + noun
eg. bhuku + "nde" + rechikoro = bhuku nde rechikoro (the book is for school)

2. "is for the purpose of":
"nde" + noun conjugation[re/ye/dze/e/we/che/zve] + infinitive verb
eg. bhuku + "nde" + "re" + kuverenga = bhuku nde rekuverenga (the book is for the purpose of reading)

The following examples illustrate the above rule:

Bhora **nde re**musangano
The ball is for the [political] party

Chitoro **nde che**kutengesa bhutsu
The store is for selling shoes

Mwana **nde wa**ngu
The child is mine

Vana ava **nde va**ngu
These children are mine

Vanhu avo **nde ve**kuSouthAfrica
Those people are South African[49]

[49]The literal translation, of course, is "those people are for South Africa", but "are for", in this context, means, "from". This is a common way of saying "from [some country]" in Shona. Recall, however, that you can also use the verb "-bva", meaning "come from" (for example, vanobva kuSouth Africa – they come from South Africa).

Mabhodhoro **nde e**doro
The bottles are for beer

Imbwa **nde dzeku**chengeta pamba
The dogs are there for the purpose of guarding the house

When combined with "kuti", the phrase comes to mean "is that" or, in rare circumstances, "about", as the rule box shows.

Rule: nde [re/ye/dze/e/we/che/zve] kuti – is that...
"nde" + noun conjugation[re/ye/dze/e/we/che/zve] + kuti
eg. dambudziko + "nde" + "re" + "kuti" haana mari = dambudziko nde rekuti haana mari (The problem is that he doesn't have money)

For example:

Pundutso yekushandisa motokaryi iyo **nde yekuti** haifi
The advantage of using that car is that it doesn't break down

Dambudziko **nde rekuti** hapana anoziva kuti chipatara chirikupi
The problem is that nobody knows where the hospital is

Mudzi wenyaya **nde we**kuti vanhu avo havana kunzwisisa nezve mamiriro ezvinhu
The root of the matter **is that** those people haven't understood the situation

Chinonakidza **nde chekuti** iye pachake ane huori
The interesting thing **is that** he himself is corrupt

Musangano **nde wekuti** tingaderedze marara sei munzvimbo ino
The meeting is about[50] how we reduce litter in this area

[50]Note that in the case of talking about a meeting, "ndewe kuti" translates to "about" rather than "is that".

Like you, like him, like her, like them, like us

Using "like" to make a comparison to a person requires using "se" (like) together with an absolute pronoun. These combinations, however, are often clumsy and are abbreviated to a shorter version, as the below table shows:

English	**Shona**	**Shona (abbreviated)**
Like me	se + ini	seni
Like you (s)	se + iwe	sewe
Like you (pl)	se + imi	semi
Like him/her	se + iye	saye
Like us	se + isu	sesu
Like them	se + ivo	savo

Examples:

Ndinoona kuti anofunga **seni**
I see that she thinks **like me**

imbavha **sewe**
he/she is a thief **like you**

Vakangwara **semi**
They are intelligent **like you** (plural)

Vane mhanza **saye**[51]
They are lucky **like him**

Anorwadzwa pamwoyo **sesu**
He suffers from heartache **like us**

[51]Note that "mhanza" (luck) in Shona is a noun and is therefore conjugated with the verb to have. In English, however, lucky is a state that is referred to using the verb "to be".

Anoda kutonga **savo**
He wants to rule **like them**

Weather, climate and time

In Shona weather and climate are described with the present continuous tense or the verb "to have". The present continuous is used when using verbs and the verb "to have", when referring to nouns.

For example, nhasi kuri kupisa means "today it is hot" but, in fact, translates literally as "today it is being hot".

When describing weather using a noun like "wind" or "cloud", the verb "to have" is used. "Nhasi kune mhepo" translates literally to "today has wind" or, more accurately in English, as "today is windy".

Examples of common descriptions are:

Mwedzi uno kune mabhanan'ana akawanda
This month there is a lot of thunder

Gore rino kune nzara
This year there is a drought

Gore rinouya kuchange kune magutwa
Next year there will be abundance

Nhasi usiku kune nyenyedzi zhinji
This evening there are many stars

Nhasi usiku hakuna[52] nyenyedzi zhinji
This evening there aren't many stars

Mwedzi uno hakuna chando
This month it isn't cold

[52]Note that the verb "to have" in this case is used in the negative in exactly the same way as outlined in the first book of the series, "Zero to functional in 12 lessons".

Vhiki rakapera kwakanga[53] kune makore
Last week was cloudy

Nezuro usiku kwakanga kune rima
Last night it was dark

Mwedzi unouya kuchange[54] kune mhepo
This coming month will be windy

Vhiki rino kuri kutonhora
This week it is cold

Mwedzi wakapera kwakanga kuri kuvhuvhuta
Last month it was windy

Nezuro kwakanga kuri kunaya
Yesterday it was raining

Useful phrases

Below are some useful phrases that help to give sentences richer meaning

SOKUZIVA KWANGU - AS FAR AS I KNOW

Sokuziva kwangu, mukaka wakanwiwa vhiki rakapera
As far as I know, the milk was drunk last week

Sokuziva kwangu, hurumende yakati tinofanira kutora visa gore rino
As far as I know, the government said we have to get visas this year

Sokuziva kwangu, Baba vakaenda kuSouth Africa kundogadzira motokari
As far as I know, father went to South Africa to fix the car

[53]Recall that "kwakanga" means "it was"
[54]Recall that "kuchange" means "it will"

SOKUUDZWA KWANGU – AS FAR AS I'M TOLD

Sokuudzwa kwangu, nyika haina mayusa yakakwana
As far as I'm told, the country has insufficient US dollars

Sokuudzwa kwangu, musevenzi achauya mangwana 8am isati yasvika
As far as I'm told, the worker will come tomorrow before 8am

Embassy yeHolland yakavarwa mwedzi wakapera, sokuudzwa kwangu
The embassy of Holland was closed last month, as far as I'm told

KUNE RIMWE DIVI – ON THE ONE HAND/ON THE OTHER HAND

Kune rimwe divi, mari yeremittance iri kukura asi, **kune rimwe divi**, maindustrie enyika ari kudzikira
On the one hand, remittance money is growing but, **on the other hand**, local industry is shrinking

Kune rimwe divi, hurumende inotaura nezve kusabhadhara kuzvipatara, asi **kune rimwe** divi, hurumende inoti haina mari nekudaro vanhu vanofanira kutenga mishonga vega[55]
On the one hand, the government promotes no fees at hospitals, **but on the other hand**, says it doesn't have money and that, as such, people must pay for medicine themselves

Kune rimwe divi, bato re SACP rinotaura nezve kuwedzera masimba vanhu, asi **kune rimwe divi**, rine mapolicies anokonzera urombo[56] vanhu
On the one hand the SACP talks about empowering people**, but on the other hand**, has policies that make people poorer

---

[55]Note that "vega" means, literally, "them alone", but translates, in cases like this, to "themselves"
[56]Note that "urombo" is often used to mean "sorry", as in "ndine urombo" (I am sorry). However, keep in mind that it's true meaning is "poor". When one says, "ndine urombo", then, it means, literally, "I have poverty", where "poverty" is taken to mean "poverty of character" for having been in the wrong.

MUKATIKATI MEMWOYO WANGU - IN MY HEART OF HEARTS

Mukatikati memwoyo wangu, ndinoziva kuti ndinoda mukadzi iyeyu chete
In my heart of hearts, I know that I want that particular woman only

Ndaifunga kuti ndaisatya, asi **mukatikati memwoyo wangu**, nhasi, ndiri kuona kuti ndiri kutyira chaizvo kuti handichawana basa
I had thought that I was without fear, but **in my heart of hearts**, today, I see that I'm very afraid that I won't find work

Mukatikati mwoyo wangu, ndinovimba kuti achabudirira kubasa rake itsva
In my heart of hearts, I hope that she will do well at her new job

Nga/-ngango – let /might

In Shona "nga" is used in three different ways to mean three different things. When "nga" is used at the start of a sentence it means "let". When

Rule 1: Nga (as "let")[57]
"nga" + pronoun + modified verb
eg. "nga" + ndi + enda[58] = ngandiende (let me go)
Rule 2: -nga (as "may/can")
pronoun + "nga" + modified verb + "here"
eg. ndi + "nga" + endewo[59] here? = ndingaendewo here? (May I go)
Rule 3: -ngango ("might")
pronoun + "ngango" + verb
eg ndi + "ngango" + enda kutaundi = ndingangoenda kutaundi (I might go to town)

---

[57]Note that "let" in English can either express a mild intent to perform some action (for example "let me drive to the store"), or it can, be used to mean "permit" (for example, "for heaven's sake, Tony, let your daughter go to the dance!)" Shona uses "let" in the same intonation-dependent way.
[58]Note that the verb ending changes to "e" when used with "nga".
[59]Note that the suffix "wo" is not an absolute requirement when using "nga" (with regards to Rule 2). It is merely an optional further layer of politeness. Remember, however, that if "wo" is omitted, the ending must, as in the case of Rule 1, be adjusted with an "e".

used after the pronoun it means "may". Finally, when used after the pronoun with "ngo", means "might". The rule above clarifies the differences.

In the rule box, above, note that Rule 1 and Rule 2 are used to make requests polite. Rule 3 is used, as it is in English, to communicate a possibility.

Examples of Rule 1:

Ngatimubatsir**e**
Let us help him/her

Ngandigadziris**e** motokari nechipanera
Let me fix the car with the spanner

Ngavasimudz**e** mapango netambo
Let them raise the planks with the rope

Ngaatyair**e** motokari itszva
Let him/her drive the new car

Ngatinamatire kuregerewa
Let us pray for forgiveness

Ngandizadze bhaketi nemvura
Let me fill the bucket with water

Examples of Rule 2

Note that with the examples below, that the tonality of the voice will indicate that permission is being requested, regardless of whether or not "here" is included at the end of the statement.

Ndingagez**ewo** motokari?
May I wash the car?

Tingabhadar**ewo** bhiri here?
May we pay this bill?

Ndingapamhidzir**ewo** mafungiro matsva padocument here?
May I add new ideas to the document?

Tingatumidz**e** zita rekuti chii?
What name can we call it?

Mungapedzis**e** kutaura pafoni here?
Would you finish off talking on the phone?

Vangatungidz**e** stove here?
May they light the stove?

Examples of Rule 3
Ndingangogeza motokari pazororo rino
I might wash the car this holiday

Tingangoswera kuDomboshawa musi weMugovera
We might spend the day at Domboshawa on Saturday

Vangangodzidza tsika itsva kuNicaragua mwedzi uno
They might learn some new customs in Nicaragua this month

Angangozviuraya pamusoro penhamo
He/she might commit suicide because of poverty

Tingangogona kugadzirisa motokari yedu kugaraji ikoko
We might be able to fix our car at that garage

Vangangowana mari kuATM pedyo neBorrowdale
They might find money at the ATM near Borrowdale

kufunga nezve (to think about)/kufungira kuti (to think that)

In English we often discuss ideas by saying things like "I am thinking about [some idea]", or "I am thinking that [some action will take place] ", or "I am thinking of [someone or some place]". In many instances the three phrases are interchangeable, but there are also many instances in which there are subtle differences in meaning between the phrases.

"Thinking about" something, for example, usually suggests that there is some depth to the thought. In that regard it would make more sense to say "Johnny is thinking about Quantum Mechanics" rather than "Johnny is thinking of Quantum Mechanics".

"Thinking of" something, in contrast, suggests that a thought is shallow or ephemeral. "I thought of you", for example, suggests a brief and non-profound thought, one that might occur after seeing some gift in a store window.

"Thinking that" usually suggests the existence of an assumption about some action, predicated on a stated or unstated condition. "I am thinking that I may go to town if it doesn't rain", for example, suggests that going to town will happen under the stated condition that it doesn't rain. Likewise, in the statement "I think that he's unlikely to hold down a good job", there is an embedded assumption that the person in question will be unable to hold down a good job under an unstated condition (such as having a bad attitude towards work, for example).

In Shona, "thinking about" best translates to "kunfunga nezve", and "thinking that" is best translated as "kufungira kuti".

The following examples should make the idea clearer:

Ndiri **kufungira kuti** ndingaenda kutaundi nhasi masikati
I am **thinking that** I might go to town this afternoon

Mazuva ano **vanofunga** chaizvo **nezve** bhuku rinonzi Sapiens
These days they **think** a lot **about** a book called Sapiens

Ndiri **kufungira kuti** havagoni kudzosera motokari pamusoro pekutadza kuwana petrol
I am **thinking that** they'll be unable to return the car because of failing to find petrol

Tichа**funga** manheru **nezve** kuti tichaenda ikoko here
We will think this evening about whether we will go there

Vakati vakanga **vari kufunga nezve** hupfumi hwakatadza sei?
They said there were thinking about why the economy failed

Ano**fungira kuti** achava nemhanza gore rino
He **thinks that** he will be lucky this year

Hapana **anofungira kuti** achafa necancer
No one **thinks that** they will die of cancer

Dzimwe nguva ndino**funga nezve** ndichabudirira nedegree yangu
Sometimes I **think about** how I will succeed with my degree

Making nouns from verbs

Many nouns in English are formed from verbs. For example, the verb "weld" is modified with an "er" to describe the person, the welder, who does the welding. Other examples of nouns from verbs in English are:

Verb	**Noun**
sail	sail**er**
plumb	plumb**er**
run	runn**er**
write	writ**er**

The practice of adding "er", however, has many exceptions (for example, "cook", the verb, and "cook", the noun).

In Shona the principle of converting verbs to nouns is the same as in English, though the rules for doing so are different. In Shona, for example, a verb is converted to a noun exclusively by adding a prefix rather than a suffix.

Verbs are converted to nouns that describe humans using the "mu/va" prefix. Non-human nouns are created by using the universal "chi/zvi" prefix and, finally, abstract nouns are sometimes (but not always) created by using the prefix "ru".

The rule box below shows how these prefixes (and their corresponding endings) are applied to verbs:

Rule 1: mu/va (humans)
"mu/va" + verb + "i"
"mu" + dzidzisa[60] + "i" = mudzidzisi (teacher)

Rule 2: chi/zvi (non humans)
"chi/zvi" + verb + "o"
"chi" + dzidza + "o" = chidzidzo (lesson)

Rule 3: "ru" (abstract)
"ru" + verb + "o"
eg: "ru" + chengetedza + "o" = ruchengetedzo (maintenance)

Note that the rules above do not apply to passive verbs, which, for some reason, always end in "a". The rule is otherwise similar (see examples below).

The table below illustrates the above rules for a variety of verbs:

verb	prefix	noun
mhanya (run)	mu/va	**mu**mhany**i** (runner)
tsvaira (sweep)	mu/va	**va**tsvair**i** (sweepers)

[60]Note that the final vowel of the verb is always dropped.

tsvairiswa (make swept)	chi/zvi	**zvi**tsvairiswa**a**[61] (brooms)
tenga (buy)	chi/zvi	**chi**tengo (something that is bought)
tengesa (sell)	mu/va	**va**tengesi (shop keepers)
dzidza (learn)	mu/mi	**mu**dzidz**i** (student)
dzidza (learn)	chi/zvi	**chi**dzidz**o** (lesson)
dzidzisa (teach)	mu/va	**mu**dzidzisi (teacher)
ziva (know)	ru	**ru**ziv**o** (knowledge)
ziva (know)	chi/zvi	**zvi**ziv**o** (things that are known)
zivisa (make [something known])	chi/zvi	**chi**zivis**o** (announcement)
redza (fish)	mu/va	**va**redzi (fishermen)
redza (fish)	chi/zvi	**chi**redzo (fishing hook)
redza (fish)	ru	**ru**redzo (fishing [technique])
tambudza (to cause suffering)	mu/va	**mu**tambudzi (abuser)
tambudza (to cause suffering)	ru	**ru**tambudzo (system causing suffering)
tambudzika (to be suffering)	mu/va	**mu**tambudziki (someone who suffers)
chengetedza (keep)	ru	**ru**chengetedzo (maintenance)
namata (pray)	mu/va	**mu**namati (one who prays)
namata (pray)	chi/zvi	**chi**namato (prayer)
famba (walk)	mu	**mu**fambi (traveller)
vaka (build)	mu/va	**mu**vaki (builder)
vakisa (build [with])	chi/zvi	**zvi**vakiso (building materials)
rima (plough)	mu/va	**mu**rimi (farmer)
rimwa (be ploughed)	chi/zvi	**chi**rimwa (crop)
batsira (help)	mu/va	**mu**batsiri (helper)
batsira (help)	chi	**chi**batsiro (advice)
vimba (to have hope)	mu/va	**mu**vimbi (someone who is trusting)
vimbika (to be trustworthy)	mu/va	**va**vimbiki (trustworthy people)

[61]Note that "tsvairiswa" is a passive verb and that its corresponding noun therefore ends in "a" rather than the usual "o" seen with non-passive verbs.

Exercises

1. Convert the following verbs into their reciprocal form and use them in a sentence:
    a. Ona
       Eg. Tichaona**na** mangwana kuchikoro
    b. Dzidzisa
    c. Tuka
    d. Seka
    e. Takura
    f. -pa
    g. Dhuma
    h. Guma
2. Translate the following sentences into Shona:
    a. I will cook sadza for **myself** at the house
       Ndicha**zvi**bikira sadza pacha**ngu** kumba
    b. You will buy **yourself** clothes at the end of the month
    c. He drove the car to the store by **himself**
    d. They fixed the toilet by themselves
    e. They sometimes wash **themselves** in the river
    f. On returning to the mountain, he roasted the rabbit for **himself**
    g. When we see elephants we kill **ourselves** running[62]
    h. She was full of praise for **herself**
    i. When cutting the vegetables he accidentally cut **himself**
3. Translate the following sentences into English:
    a. Aramba kundipa makeys
       She refused to give me the keys
    b. Ndicharamba kuenda ikoko
    c. Vanoramba kuteerera mudzidzisi
    d. Munoramba muchifamba kusvikira paGiveway
    e. Ndicharamba ndichinamatira kupora kwemunin'ina wangu

[62]Note that there is an expression in Shona for "killing yourself" by doing some activity. In this case "killing yourself running" is an expression, similar to what you might find in English, emphasizing the rigour with which the running is being carried out.

f. Ndinomuda asi anoramba achindiramba

g. Pakupedza kuverenga bhuku iro, ndicharamba kuriverenga zvakare

h. Vakanga varikuramba kukwira bhazi

i. Vakanga vachingoramba vachiverenga bepanhau kudzidza nezve nyaya dzehupfumi

j. Vakaramba vachitsvaga bepanhau

4. Translate the following into Shona using either "kupfura" or "pane":

a. I like that car more than the other one
Ndinoda motokari iyo **kupfura** motokari iyo

b. I like this person more than that one

c. There are more trees here than in South Africa

d. Our economy is smaller nowadays than long ago

e. Tall people are more likely to get cancer than short people

f. This carving is more beautiful than that one

g. My life is better now than it was last year

h. These dresses are more expensive here than in town

5. Translate the following into Shona using "like this" or "like that" where necessary:

a. Remove the rotten areas from the vegetables with the knife, **like this**

Eg. Bvisai nzvimbo dzakaora pamiriwo nebanga, **se izvi**

b. As far as I'm told, you examine the stomach of the patient using the stethoscope, like this

c. Mix the eggs with the oil, like that

d. Cut the wire with the pliers, like that

e. Put the potatoes and the butternut into the oven, like this

f. Lift the lintel onto the wall, like that

g. Spray the seedlings with chemicals, like this

h. As far as I know, you attach the rope to the pole, like this

6. Translate the following into Shona, with special reference to using what you learned about "like him/her/them etc":

a. She is beautiful like you
Eg. Akanaka **sewe**

b. You are a liar, like her

c. They sometimes fail to fulfill their dreams, like us
d. On the one hand, I drive to work early, like him, but on the other, I always arrive late, like him
e. They drink a lot, like us
f. You sing very well, like them
g. I like to win, like you
h. They like to eat at restaurants, like us

7. Make the following verbs into nouns using (mu/va or chi/zvi) and translate them into English:
   a. Eg. Nyora (va)
      Vanyori - writers
   b. Nyorisa (zvi)
   c. Shamisa (chi)
   d. Tyaira (mu)
   e. Tema (mu)
   f. Tuwina (va)
   g. Kwira (va)
   h. Bika (zvi)
   i. Veza (chi)

Vocabulary

-batsira	help
-batsirana	help each other
-chengetedza	keep/look after
-dhuma	bump
-dhumana	bump into each other
-dhumana	crash into each other
-dzidzisa	teach
-dzidzisana	teach each other
-dzikira	– to reduce/shrink
-funga	think/miss
-fungana	miss each other
-geza	wash
-gezana	wash each other
-gotcha	braai/barbecue/roast
-itirana	do [to] each other

-kudza	to respect
-kudzana	to respect each other
-mhoresa	greet
-mhoresana	greet each other
-namata	pray
-netsa	bother
-netsana	bother each other
-ngwara	clever (used statively)
-ona	see
-onana	see each other
-pa	give
-panana	give each other
-pfura	shoot/pass
-pfurana	shoot/pass each other
-pora	heal/cool down
-pukuta	wipe/clean with a cloth
-redza	fish
-regerewa	be forgiven
-rova	hit
-rovana	hit each other
-rumbidza	to praise
-runga	stir
-seka	laugh
-sekana	laugh at each other
-takura	carry
-takurana	carry each other
-tambudza	cause suffering
-tengesa	sell
-tengesana	sell each other [out]
-tonhora	cold
-tuka	scold
-tukana	scold each other
-tuma	send
-tumana	send each other
-tumidza	call something [some name]
-tungidza	strike a match/light a fire
-uraya nekumhanya	to kill by running
-vhota	vote
-vimba	hope
-vimbika	be trustworthy

-wedzera masimba	empower
-zviuraya	kill oneself (ie commit suicide)
bhaketi	bucket
bhande	belt
chando	cold
chidzidzo	lesson
chinamato	prayer
chinonakidza	an interesting thing
chiredzo	fishing hook
chirimwa	crop
chitengo	something bought
chitsvairiswa	broom
chivezwa	carving
chiziviso	announcement
chizivo	something known
dhakwa	drunk
doro	beer
garaji	garage
grovo	glove
hwahwa	alcohol
kune rimwi divi	on the one hand/on the other hand
kusabhadhara	without paying
mamiriro ezvinhu	situation
Masimba	strengths
mhepo	wind
mubatsiri	helper
mudzidzi	student
mufambi	traveller
muhoro	salary
mumhanyi	runner
munamati	one who prays
muredzi	fisherman
murimi	farmer
mutambudziki	one who suffers
mutengesi	shop keeper
mutsvairi	sweeper
muvaki	builder
muvimbi	someone trustworthy
muvimbiki	trustworthy person
nhamo	poverty

nharo	argument
nyenyedzi	stars
pamhidzira	add (can be used interchangeably with "wedzera")
ponji	puncture
pundutso	advantage (noun)
rima	darkness
ruchengetedzo	maintenance
ruredzo	fishing techniques/methods
rutambudzo	system causing suffering
ruzha	noise
ruzivo	knowledge
tambo	rope
tsika	customs
vhuvhuta	wind
yusa	US dollar
zadzisa	fulfill
zvirimwa	plants
zviroto	dreams
zvisina njodzi	safely (literally: without danger)
zvivakiso	building materials

Lesson 9

IDIOMS, EXPRESSIONS AND PROVERBS

Idioms, expressions and proverbs

Shona speakers frequently use idioms when they speak. Shona proverbs, however, tend to be used less commonly nowadays, particularly in urban settings, though they are still used in rural areas. In this chapter we discuss commonly used idioms and proverbs that will take your use of Shona to the next level.

According to Wikipaedia an idiom is "a phrase or fixed expression that has a figurative, or sometimes literal, meaning"[63]. For example, "the ball is in your court", means "it is up to you to make the next decision or step".

The list of idioms and proverbs in Shona is huge. We present here a few commonly used ones. Note that there are often strong parallels with English ones.

Observe, below, that "ane" ("he/she is") is sometimes used with idioms and proverbs. This third person should be thought of as it is in old English. "Anopinda anorwara", for example, means, literally, "he gets in he gets sick" but should be thought of as "he who gets in is he who becomes sick". This form of "he/she who does this is he/she who becomes/does/befalls that" is a common motif in the language. People with an English tongue need practice and exposure to understand and apply this form of language correctly.

The proverbs and idioms given in this lesson are a good introduction to this "old English" means of relating actions to outcomes. The idioms and proverbs here are the most common, but are by no means exhaustive.

Aiva madziva ava mazambuko

What were big rivers will become crossing places

Meaning: Varies depending on context. Can mean that odds which seem insurmountable will become surmountable. The phrase can also refer to those with power, losing it.

[63]https://en.wikipedia.org/wiki/Idiom

Bofu rikati ndinokurova, rinenge rine charakatsika

If a blind person says "I hit you", he has something that he's stepping on [ie concealing]

Meaning: If someone seemingly weaker than yourself threatens you, be aware that they are concealing something important that they can and will use against you.

Chisi[64] chako masimba mashoma

Something is not yours, the powers are less

Meaning: If a possession is not yours, you have no power over it.

Chapinda kamwe hachiteerwi

A thing that has entered once will not be followed

Meaning: Something that you have seen only once does not give you a sufficient sample size to make a valid judgment. The saying is similar to "one swallow does not a summer make".

Mbada isati yadya vana vayo inotanga yavapomera kuti vanonhuwa sembudzi

Before a leopard devours her own young, she first accuses them of smelling like goats.

Meaning: People will find justifications to do what suits them

Chembere mukadzi hazvienzani nekurara mugota[65]

[Having] an old woman is not the same as sleeping in a *gota*.

Meaning: It is better to have something than nothing.

---

[64]"Chisi" is short hand for "chinhu hachisi".

[65]A "gota" is a room in a house reserved for juvenile, unmarried boys. Boys living in a "gota" have not yet found a wife. Once a boy finds a wife, he moves into his own homestead, referred to as "musha". The idea and practice of a "gota" is seemingly common in rural villages but not in towns.

Nyamunatsi ndiye nyakubayiwa

A nice person is the same person who gets stabbed

Meaning: No good deed goes unpunished. Nice guys come in last.

Chidyamatoo akadzipwa neganda remhuru

A person who eats animal skin was choked by the skin of a calf

Meaning: Even an expert can make foolish errors

Chirambakuudzwa[66] akaonekwa nembonje pahuma

A person who refuses to be given advice was seen with a wound on the forehead

Meaning: People who don't take advice end up in difficulty

Chidembo hachivhuyiwi pane vanhu vazhinji

A civet cat[67] cannot be skinned where many people are

Meaning: Information can spread inaccurately and cause problems. Some things are therefore best kept secret.

Ane bhapu

He/she has lungs

Meaning: that person can't keep a secret

---

[66]Note that some words in Shona referring to people begin with "chi". This "chi" is short for "chinhu" meaning "thing", but it nevertheless refers to a person, much like how "it" (in English) can refer to a lawyer, or doctor or some other kind of person.
[67]A dead civet cat is considered to have a terrible smell

Gumbo mumba, gumbo panze

One leg in the house and one leg outside

Meaning: the person is promiscuous or not trustworthy

Kuvaka danga pasina mombe

Building a kraal without the cattle

Meaning: Trying to run before walking

Kukanda mapfumo pasi

Throw spears down

Meaning: throwing the towel in

Kushaya ganda kumeso

Not having skin on the face

Meaning: Having no shame

Hari yofanzirofa

A clay pot that is weathered, cracked and near to the end of its use

Meaning: A very old person, about to die, hanging by a thin thread of life

Kubereka gotsi

Carrying the back of your head

Meaning: Running very fast, similar to "as fast as our legs could carry us"

Kupinda nemwenje mudziva

Entering with a light in the river[68]

Meaning: Embarking on something that will end in certain disaster.

Kudzipwa neganda nyama iripo

Being choked on skin [while] meat is there

Meaning: Wasting your time on minor and irrelevant issues to the detriment of larger and more important ones

Kutamba nemoto

Playing with fire

Meaning: the same as in English

Kutambisa miseve kumakunguo hanga dzichauya

Wasting your arrows on crows [before] the guineafowl come

Meaning: Being foolish with resources and not planning for the future, or being shortsighted and getting distracted by immediate goals to the detriment of larger, more important ones

Kuwana pashoma kuri nani pane kushaya

Half a loaf is better than none

Meaning: as in English. Having something, even if not ideal, is better than having nothing at all

[68]The idea with this idiom is that the river will make the candle wet and extinguish its flame, making navigation impossible and danger and disaster inevitable.

Kudziya moto wembavha

Warming yourself on a thief's fire

Meaning: benefiting from the dishonest actions of others undermines your own moral authority. It can also mean that you're getting yourself in above your head on something you don't fully understand

Kudzingirira mhepo

To chase the wind

Meaning: to waste your time on superfluous activities

Kufa nechekuchera

To die by your own digging

Meaning: to dig your own grave

Kudzingirira tsuro mbiri

Chasing two rabbits at once

Meaning: embarking on an impossible challenge

Kunhongwa neatanga

To be picked by whoever is the first

Meaning: the early bird gets the worm

Moyo, muti unomera paunoda

The heart, [just like a] tree, grows where it wants

Meaning: We often don't have control over our feelings

Seka urema wafa

Laugh at disability when you're dead

Meaning: Don't make fun of those less fortunate than yourself

Kudzidza hakuperi

Learning does not end

Kutsva kwendebvu varume vanodzimurana

[When someone's beard] burns, [other] men will help to extinguish the flames

Meaning: We ought to help those in need

Ari kutsi kwehope

He/she is in a deep sleep

Meaning: He/she is not paying attention to anything going on around them

Chinoziva ivhu kuti mwana wembeva anorwara

What knows is the soil that the young of a mouse is sick

Meaning: Only insiders know the true state of affairs

Abaiwa ngabude

He [who has been] stabbed can leave

Meaning: if you feel the conditions are bad, you are always free to leave

Mwana asingachemi anofira mumbereko

A child who doesn't cry dies in the cradle

Meaning: People should not suffer in silence

Tototenda maruva tadya shakata

We believe in the [plant's] blossoms when we've eaten the fruit

Meaning: Promises are not to be relied on until they've been kept

Kurera imbwa nemukaka mangwana inofuma yokuruma

Bring up a dog on milk and it bites you the next day

Meaning: A dog bites the hand that feeds it

Mugoni wemwana ndiye asinaye

The one who can manage a child is the one without [one]

Meaning: People think that difficult tasks are easy if they've never done them

Ane ganda ane nyama hazvienzani neakabata howa

He who has skin has [at least some] meat, [and this] is not the same as [him] holding a mushroom

Meaning: Half a loaf is better than none

Nhembwe rudzi kuzvara mwana ane kazhumu

A duiker is the species if it has a child he [the child] will have a goats beard

Meaning: A chip off the old block/ like father, like son

Nyamunatsi ndiye nyamutsingwa

The person who does good is the [one who becomes the] injured person

Meaning: People who do good deeds are often the first to be taken advantage of

Chara chimwe hachitswanyi inda

One finger is unable to crush a louse

Meaning: Some problems require many people to overcome them

Gore haribvi pakabva rimwe

The year doesn't pass like the one before

Meaning: Don't expect the future to be like the past

Mukuru mukuru hanga haigari papfunde

An elder is an elder, a guineafowl cannot sit on the sorghum [vine]

Meaning: Respect your elders. In this analogy, an elder is always an elder, and therefore, as an analogy with a guineafowl, will always cause the vine to bend when it sits on it. This implies that the elder will always understand more or have more impact on his/her surroundings than younger people.

Majongwe maviri haariri pamutanda mumwe chete

Two cockerels cannot crow on the same log

Meaning: You can't have two bulls in the same padock

Kandiro kanoenda kunobva kamwe

A small plate goes where the other one comes from

Meaning: You scratch my back and I'll scratch yours. In Shona culture, when you are given something by a neighbor you often give an equivalent gift in return. In the saying, above, then, the plate is given with one kind of food on it, but given back by the other person with another kind of food on it. The saying speaks of the necessity of reciprocity.

Manenji kuti gudo ripunzike mumuti

[it is] unexpected that the baboon falls from the tree

Meaning: We don't expect experts to make mistakes

Ateya mariva murutsva haachatyi kusviba magaro

He who sets traps on the burned grass will not be afraid to get dirty from the soot

Meaning: You can't always pick and choose

Exercises

1. Translate the following sentences into Shona:
    a. The woman doesn't pay taxes and, therefore, is **playing with fire**
    Mukadzi habhadari matexes, saka **ari kutamba nemoto**
    b. On seeing the hyena we ran as fast as our legs could carry us
    c. I left that woman because she isn't trustworthy
    d. I'm angry with my friend because he's got a big mouth
    e. I tried to beat him but I eventually threw the towel in
    f. She often asked for money because she had no shame
    g. I went to see grandmother last month, and she was hanging on to life by a thread
    h. Fixing the radiator when the engine is broken is a pointless waste of time
2. Finish off the following common idioms and proverbs
    a. Ane ganda ane nyama ____________________
    b. Kunhongwa ________
    c. Moyo, muti unomera ________
    d. Gumbo mumba, __________
    e. ______ nemoto
    f. _________ ndiye nyakubayiwa
    g. _________ ava mazambuko
    h. Mbada isati yadya vana vayo inotanga ___________________

Vocabulary

-bayiwa	get stabbed
-dzimura	extinguish [fire]
-dzingirira	chase
-dzipwa	be choked
-kanda	throw
-mera	grow/germinate
-nhongwa	be picked
-nhuwa	smell [like something]
-rera	raise [young ones]
-rira	sing/crow
-sviba	get dirty
-tambisa	waste
-tsinga	hurt/cripple
bhapu	lungs
bofu	blind person
chara	finger
chidembo	civet cat
chidyamatoo	a meat eater
chirambakuudzwa	a person who refuses advice
chisi	something that isn't yours
danga	kraal
ganda	skin
gotsi	back of the head
hari	traditional clay pot
howa	mushroom
huma	forehead
inda	louse
jongwe	cockerel

kandiro	small plate
kazhumu	goat's beard
kutsi	deep
madziva	fast flowing rivers
magaro	soot
makunguo	crows
manenji[69]	unexpected happening
mariva	traps
mbereko	cradle
mbeva	mouse
mbonje	deep impact wound
mhuru	calf
mugoni	an expert
mukuru	elder
museve	arrow
mutanda	log
mwenje	light
ndebvu	beard
nhembwe	duiker
nyamunatsi	kind/good person
nyamutsingwa	injured person
pfunde	sorghum
rudzi	species or variety
shakata	wild fruit
urema	disability
zumbuko	crossing place

[69]This idea of an "unexpected happening" is often taken to refer to a taboo activity

Lesson 10

COMMON SITUATIONS

Common situations

In this chapter we examine a number of situations that are likely to be encountered in Zimbabwe. These situations include building and renovating, running a middleclass household, navigating airport customs officials, engaging in rural development work, and, finally, looking at some medical situations that might be encountered by a rural doctor.

Building and renovating a house

Below we examine a case in which someone is in the process of instructing workers to build a small cottage, using cement, bricks, lintels and other components.

Situation background: You are engaging James, a builder, to renovate a cottage. This includes knocking down some walls, building new walls, adding a verandah and preparing the bathroom for a plumber who will come in when the initial construction is complete.

	Shona	**English**
You	Mangwanani James. Mune zvinhu zvese zvaunoda zvekutanga kuvaka here?	Morning James. Do you have everything you need to start building?
James	Ehe. Ndine zvese kunze kwe pitsand. Iri kuuya rini?	Yes. I have everything except pitsand. When is it coming?
You	Ndataura naTendai nhasi mangwanani. Ati achauya netruck kuma 1pm. Iri bho here?	I spoke with Tenda this morning. He said he would come with his truck at 1pm. Is that okay?
James	Ehe	Yes
You	Zvakajeka here zvatakawiriranа zvekuita pano?	Is what we agreed on doing here clear?

James	Ehe. Wakati tinofanira kubvisa madziro aya, kuvaka madziro maviri, kusimudza malintel matatu, uye kuchera mafoundation yeveranda	Yes. You said we must remove these walls, build two walls, erect 3 lintels and dig foundations for the verandah.
You	Good	Zvakanaka

After some hours you return to the building site and discover that a variety of things are not being done correctly. Two of the lintels have not been put in straight and the foundations being built for the verandah are not deep enough. You set about correcting James and his team on their errors.

	Shona	**English**
You	Pachipamwe. Ndaona mamwe mamistake pamalintel uye pa mafoundation uye pamadziro.	Hi. I have seen some mistakes with the lintels, the foundation and the walls.
James	Mamistake akadii?	What kind of mistakes?
You	Pekutanga malintel aya haana kuenzana. Munofanira kubvisa uye kusimudza zvakare. Mashandisa spirit level here?	To begin with these lintels here are not level. You must remove them and erect them again. Did you use a spirit level?
James	Ehe, asi haisi kushanda zvakanaka	Yes but it doesn't work properly
You	Iyezvino shandisa spirit level yangu.	This time use my spirit level
James	Ko, pamafoundation?	How about the foundations?

You	Ndakati munofanira kuchera 75cm asi machera nhasi 50cm chete. Saka, ndinoda kuti mudzikise.	I said that you should dig the foundations to 75cm but you dug them only to 50cm. Therefore I want you to deepen them.
James	Ko, madziro ari sei?	And the walls, how are they?
You	Ndaona zvinhu zviviri. Chekutanga, hamuna kusefa pitsendi. Onai mashizha neuswa musemendi. Chechipiri hamuna kuvaka madziro akaswatuka. Saka munofanira kuputsa madziro ese uye kutanga zvakare.	I saw two things. First, you didn't sieve the pitsand. Look at these leaves and grass in the cement. Second, you didn't build the walls straight. Therefore, you will need to knock them all down and start again.
James	Muchawedzera zvishoma here?	Will you pay me a little more [for redoing the work]?
You	Kwete. Mucontract makanyorwa kuti handiwedzeri mari kana makanganisa zvatakawirirana.	No. In the contract it's written that I do not pay more money if you make an error regarding that which we agreed.
James	Zvakanaka. Pakupedza mabasa aya, tinofanira kuita chii?	okay. On finishing these tasks here what must we do?
You	Tangai kuvaka bathroom	Please start to build the bathroom

James and his team eventually finish the walls and straighten the lintels. We next catch up with the process when the bathroom is being inspected.

	Shona	**English**
You	Makorokoto, maita floor zvakanaka. Asi ndinoona kuti maplugholes ese akakwira. Onai! Mvura haisi kugona kufamba nokuti level yemaplugs yakakwira pane level yemvura pachayo. Munofanira kudzikisa maplug ne3cm.	Well done, you did the floors well. However, I see that all the plugholes are raised. Look here! The water is unable to flow because the level of the plugs is higher than the water itself. You must lower the plugs by 3cm.
James	Zvakanaka. Pakupedza mabasa aya, ndinogona here kutanga kutiler?	Very well. On finishing this work, can I start tiling?
You	Usati watanga kutiler munofanira kusiya nzvimbo yekuisa mapipe. Tangai kutiler mangwana.	Before you start tiling you must leave space for putting the pipes. Start with the tiling tomorrow.

Dealing with a domestic worker

In Zimbabwe many middleclass people have workers that come in to do household work or gardening. The situation presented here assumes that you are living in a house with two children, and have a maid and a gardener who help twice a week.

We begin the dialogue when Rudo (the house helper) turns up for work. For the sake of brevity we begin after the initial greetings have been made.

	Shona	English
You	Nhasi tangai nendiro. Nezuro masikati ndakaisa mbatya dzakawanda muwashing machine. Bvisai uye nanikai paline panze. Dzisati dzanyatsooma dzibvisei[70] paline uye tangai kuaina.	Today please start with the dishes. Yesterday afternoon I put lots of clothes in the washing machine. Please remove them and dry them outside on the line. Before they're completely dry, remove them from the line and begin ironing.
Rudo	Zvakanaka. Ndiratidzei mashandisiro ayo	Very well. Please show me how it works.
You	Zvakanaka. Kutanga, munoisa sipo shoma yepowder munzvimbo iyi se izvi. Pashure, munosarudza setting yekuwacha cotton (dzimwe nguva munogona kusarudza synthetics kana wool). Pakupedzisira, munodzvinya "start" button. Zvaita.	Very well. To start, you put a little soap powder in this place like this. After, you choose the setting for washing cotton. (Other times you might choose synthetics or wool.) Finally, you push the "start" button. It's done.

Later you ask Rudo to clean and polish a few things about the house and then prepare for the children arriving home from school:

	Shona	English
You	Gezai motokari. Dzinofanira kuchena nokuti shamwari yangu anoda kudzikwereta.	Please wash the cars. They need to be clean[71] because a friend wants to borrow them. After

[70]When the object infix "dzi" is used to refer to clothes, here, note that the ending is modified from "ai" to "ei".

[71]In English "and they must be clean" might sound abrupt and perhaps impolite. In Shona, so long as the "ai" ending is used for the main verb (in this case "geza) then the sentence maintains its politeness.

	Pashure pekugeza, pukutai nejira. Uye zorai polish. Pashure pe5 minutes, shayinisai nejira rakachena.	washing them, dry them with a cloth. And apply polish. After 5 minutes shine with a clean cloth.
Rudo	Asi polish yakatopera	But the polish is finished
You	Zvakanaka. Ndichaitenga masikati. Asi munguva inotevera munofanira kundizivisa zvinhu zvisati zvapera.	Very well. I will buy it this afternoon. But in future let me know before things run out.
Rudo	Zvakanaka	
You	Ndichatora vana kuchikoro kuma 1pm. Bikai hove nemapotato, uye gadzirai salad ne madomasi, lettuce, maonyeni uye red pepper. Shandisai grater kuisa cheese pamusoro pesalad zvishoma.	I will collect the children from school at 1pm. Please cook fish and potatoes, prepare the salad with tomatoes, lettuce, onions and red pepper. Use the grater to put a little cheese on top of the salad.
Rudo	Hove dziri kupi?	Where are the fish?
You	Dziri mufiriji mupantry pashelf yepazasi[72].	They're in the fridge in the pantry on the bottom shelf.
You	Pashure pekutora vana ndiri kuenda chitoro. Manyora here shopping list?	After I fetch the kids I'm going to the store. Have you written a shopping list?

[72] "Top shelf" is "shelf ye pamusoro" and "middle shelf" is "shelf yepakati".

Rudo	Ehe. Tinoda mukaka, chingwa, mazai, sipho yekugezesa. Zvakanyorwa zvose palist.	Yes. We need milk, bread, eggs, bathing soap. Everything's written on the list.
You	Zvakanaka. Maita basa!	Very well. Thank you!

In the kitchen later that afternoon you are unable to find the napkins in their usual place. You ask Rudo about them.

	Shona	**English**
You	Rudo, ndaifunga kuti manep-keni ari mucupboard asi nhasi handina kumaona. Munoziva here kuti ari kupi?	Rudo, I thought that the napkins were in the cupboard but today I haven't seen them. Do you know where they are?
Rudo	Ndakaaisa mulaundry basket nezuro nokuti akasviba. Ndi-neurombo, ndakakanganwa kudzosera. Ndicha atora iyezvino.	I put them in the wash yesterday because they were dirty. I'm sorry, I forgot to return [them]. I will get them now.
You	Dziri mufiriji mupantry pashelf yepazasi[73].	They're in the fridge in the pantry on the bottom shelf.
You	Pashure pekutora vana ndiri kuenda chitoro. Manyora here shopping list?	After I fetch the kids I'm going to the store. Have you written a shopping list?

Rudo	Ehe. Tinoda mukaka, chingwa, mazai, sipho yekugezesa. Zvakanyorwa zvose palist.	Yes. We need milk, bread, eggs, bathing soap. Everything's written on the list.
You	Zvakanaka. Maita basa!	Very well. Thank you!

[73]"Top shelf" is "shelf ye pamusoro" and "middle shelf" is "shelf yepakati".

Some time later you return from the store.

	Shona	English
You	Shopping iri mumotokari	The shopping is in the motorcar
Rudo	handisi kuona sipo yekugezesa pashopping	I don't see the bath soap with the shopping
You	Ah! Ndineurombo nda-kanganwa kuitenga!	Ah! Sorry, I forgot to buy it!
Rudo	Hazvinei. Pane sipo imwechete yakasara. Munogona kutenga mangwana kana vhiki rinouya	It doesn't matter. There's a little soap left. You can buy [some more] tomorrow or next week

Dealing with a gardener

Here we look at some common gardening activities. We begin with Tapuwa coming on duty in the morning and receiving instructions about the day's activities. For brevity, greetings are once again omitted.

	Shona	English
You	Nhasi munofanira kudzura sora mulawn. Pashure, cheka uswa ne lawnmower. Pashure peranji diridzai maruva ese uye isai mushonga we nhata pama-roses. Usazokanganwa kudiri-dza maruva pa mahanging-basket.	Today you must weed the lawn. Afterwards, cut the grass with the lawnmower. After lunch water all the flowers and put the aphid chemical on the roses. Finally, don't forget to water the flowers in the hanging baskets.

Tapuwa	Zvakanaka. Ndinofanira kuisa marara kupi?	Very well. Where should I put the rubbish[74]?
You	Isai marara pacompost	Put the leftover grass on the compost heap.

You inspect his work later and find that some things still need some extra attention.

You	Ndaona masora palawn kuseri kweimba. Wadzura uko here?	I saw some weeds on the lawn behind the house. Did you weed there?
Tapuwa	Handina kuwana nguva nhasi. Ndinogona kuzviita[75] mangwana here? Handisati ndaisa mushonga pamarose.	I didn't find the time today. Can I do it tomorrow? I haven't yet put the chemicals on the roses.
You	Ehe. Zviitei mangwana. Uye mangwana zvakare, temai mapazi kubva ku muti uyo, pedyo ne fenzi inemagetsi. Mapazi ne fenzi hazvifaniri kugumana.	Yes. Please do it tomorrow. Also, tomorrow, please cut the branches from that tree by the electric fence. The branch and fence should not touch each other.
Tapuwa	Ndinofanira kuita sei ne mapazi aya?	What should I do with the banches?
You	Temai zvidimbu uye unganidza pabakwa pashure pemba	Please cut them into pieces and stack them on the woodpile behind the house

[74]Note that he is talking about left over grass from the mowing but refers to it as "rubbish". In shona all discarded things regardless of their biodegradability come under the banner of "rubbish".
[75]Note that "zvi" here is an object infix that refers to the "things" that need to be done, so "ku zviita" most closely translates to "the things to do".

Tapuwa is new and in need of some training. You explain to him the following week how to plant some seeds.

	Shona	English
You	Nhasi tichadzidza nezvekusima maruva e Marigold. Kutanga munochera gomba pakati pe 8cm kusvika 12cm. Munoisa manyowa mashoma se izvi. Pashure, isai nhondo mugomba. Wedzera ivhu ye topsoil. Kana mapedza, diridzai nemvura shoma.	Today we will learn about transplanting Marigold seedlings. To start, dig a hole between 8 and 12 cm deep. Put a little manure [in the hole] like this. After, put the seedling in the hole. Fill in [the hole] with topsoil. When you're finished, irrigate with a little water.
Tapuwa	Ndinofanira kudiridza maruva kangani pavhiki?	How many times should I water per week?
You	Munodiridza ka3, mangwanani ega ega	You water three times [per week], in the mornings

Common rural medical situations

Medical situations are many and varied and a comprehensive guide to dealing with them is beyond the scope of this book. We do, however, present here a guide to dealing with the most common complaints and ailments.

The situation: You are working as a doctor for a medical NGO clinic in a remote part of Zimbabwe. Your job is to deal with sick villagers as they present themselves to you. Your first visit is from a mother who's toddler is suffering from diarrhea and vomiting.

	Shona	**English**
You	Ndiani ari kurwara?	Who is sick?
Mother	Mwana wangu	My child
You	Ane makore mangani?	How old is she?
Mother	Ane makore 5	She's 5 years old
You	Ari kunzwa chii?	What's afflicting her?
Mother	Ane manyoka uye akatanga kurutsa nezuro	She has diarrhoea and she started vomiting yesterday
You	Akatanga kuchaya rini?	When did she start with diarrhea?
Mother	marimwezuro	the day before yesterday
You	Ari kurutsa chikafu nguva dzose here?	Does she vomit every time she eats?
Mother	ehe	Yes
You	Ari kupisa muviri here?	Does she have a temperature
Mother	Handizivi	I don't know
You	Kutanga, ndichatora temperature uye ropa. Pashure, munofanira kumupa ORS kumisa kushomeka kwemvura.	To begin with I will take her temperature and [some] blood. After, I will give her ORS[76] to stop the dehydration.
Mother	Zvakanaka	Very well

[76]Oral Rehydration Solution (Dioralyte). It is often referred to as this in hospital settings in many African countries.

You	Ndichaongorora ropa kuti imararia here. Mangwana ndichakupai maresult.	I will test the blood for malaria. Tomorrow I will give you the results.
Mother	Zvakanaka	Very well
You	Zita rako ndiani?	What is your name?
Child	Zita rangu ndi Chiedza	My name is Chiedza
You	Chiedza, ndipe ruoko rwako. Uchanzwa kurwadza zvishoma	Chiedza, Please give me your arm. You'll feel a small pain.
You	Amai endai kuGreenwood Pharmacy muna Jason Moyo neprescription iyi. Vachakupai mapiritsi	Miss, please go to Greenwood Pharmacy on Jason Moyo street with this prescription. They will give you some pills.

We now look at a situation in which a 15 year old boy comes to the clinic with a bacterial infection on his thigh.

	Shona	**English**
You	Urikunzwa chii?	What's afflicting you?
Boy	Ndine mota pagumbo	I have a boil on my leg
You	Ndiratidze	Please show me
Boy	Ndinofanira kubvisa shoti yangu	I have to remove my shorts
You	Zvakanaka. Ndichadzvinyadzvinya pedyo nemota. Ndinoda kunzwa pose panorwadza. Pari kurwadza apa	Very well. I will press down near the boil. I want to test where it's painful. Is it painful here? A little or a lot or not at all?

	here? Zvishoma kana zvakanyanya kana kwete?	
Boy	Zvakanaka	Very well
You	Pari kurwadza apa here?	Is it sore here?
Boy	ehe	Yes
You	Pari kurwadza apa?	Is it sore here?
Boy	Kwete	No
You	urwa rwunombobuda here?	Does puss ever come out?
Boy	Ehe, dzimwe nguva	Yes, sometimes
You	Unombopisa zvakanyanya here?	Do you ever run a high temperature?
Boy	Ehe, mamwe mazuva	Yes, on some days
You	Urikunwa mushonga here?	Are you taking medicine?
Boy	Ehe	Yes
You	Mushonga wakadii?	What kind of medicine?
Boy	Unonzi Paracetamol	It's called Paracetamol
You	Zvakanaka. Ndinoda kukupa mumwe mushonga, unonzi Amoxycillen. Uchauraya utachiwana	Very well. I want to give you another medicine called Amoxycillen. It will kill the bacteria
Boy	Zvakanaka	Zvakanaka
You	Kutanga ndichatumbura mota. Pashure ndichaisa mushonga	To start I will lance the boil. After I will put some antiseptic on the

	Shona	English
	pachironda. Kupedzisira ndichaisa bandage. Endai kuPharmacy neprescription iyi kundotenga mapiritsi eAmoxycillin	wound. Finally I will put a bandage [on the wound]. Go to the pharmacy with this prescription and buy the Amoxycillin tablets

Finally, we look at a situation recounted by a real life doctor in the field, concerning a woman with a child suspected to be infected with HIV.

	Shona	**English**
Doctor	Ndingakubatsirai sei?	How can I help you?
Patient	Mwana wangu ane chikosoro uye arikutadza kufema zvakanaka. Arikushaya simba, haadyi kana kunwa, uye ari kuondoroka mwedzi uyu	My child has a cough and difficulty breathing. She's very weak, she doesn't eat or drink and she's lost weight this month
Doctor	Maiwe! Ngandimuongorore. Anoratidzika kuti haana simba. Anofanira kugara kuchipatara	Oh dear! Let me examine her. She does look very sick. She needs to stay in hospital
Mother	Saka ndoita sei?	So what should I do?
Doctor	Garai pano pachipatara nemwana wenyu. Ndichamupa mushonga nejekiseni, uye ndichashandisa IV kumupa mushonga wemvura	Stay here at the hospital with your child. I will give her medicine with an injection and give her some fluid through an IV
Mother	Tichagara pano nguva yakadii?	How long will we be here for?
Doctor	Handizivi, zvinoenderana nemwana wenyu kuti achatambira mushonga sei.	I don't know, it depends on your child and how she reacts to the medicine. Have you or her ever been tested for HIV or TB?

	Makambopiwa HIV test kana TB here?	
Mother	Kwete	No
Doctor	Ndinoshushikana nezve mwana wenyu. Ndinoda HIV test kwaari	I am very worried about your child. I want to do an HIV test on her.
Mother	Asi, kana ane HIV, handiti achangofa?	But if she has HIV won't she die anyway?
Doctor	Mishonga yeHIV inoshanda zvakanakisa. Inochengetedza vanhu kwemakore mazhinji mazuva ano	The medicines for HIV are very good. They keep people alive for many years nowadays
Mother	Ndinotya chaizvo, ndainzwa kuti mishonga iyi yakaipa uye inorwarisa	I am very scared, I've heard these medicines are bad and make you sick
Doctor	Munoda here kutaura nakanzura vanoshandisa mishonga yeHIV. Vanogona kutsanangura zvakanaka kuti mishonga inoshanda zvakanaka	Would you like to talk to one of our counsellors who is on HIV treatment. They will be able to explain that the medicines work well
Mother	Handisikuda kuti mwana wangu apiwe test yeHIV	I don't want my child to be given an HIV test
Doctor	Kana tichitadza kumupa test yeHIV, uye ane HIV, achafa	If we don't test her and she has HIV, she will die

Mother	Murume wangu achandirowa kana ndichiita test yeHIV kwaari	My husband will beat me if I have her tested
Doctor	Zvakakosha kuti apiwe test yeHIV, newe futi, kubatsira utano hwenyu, uye kubatsira utano hwemwana wenyu. Tine makanzura pano ekukubatsi-rai. Vaiva madambudziko akafanana nemi	It is very important to have her tested, and you too, for your own health and your other childrens' health. We have counsellors here who can help you. They have had similar experiences
Mother	Zvakanaka	Okay
Doctor	Mazviita. Tichaita test yeHIV yenyu uye mwanasikana wenyu. Ichabuda kuma 30 mi-netsi. Batai ruoko rwemwana-sikana wenyu. Ndinoda ku-mupa oxygen nemishonga neIV iyezvino.	Thank you. We will do the test now for you and your daughter. It will be ready in 30 minutes. Please hold your child's arm. I would like to give her oxygen now and medi-cines through the IV.
Mother	Zvakanaka	very well
Doctor	Kanzura vachauya manje manje kutaura nemi	The counsellor will be here shortly to talk with you
Mother	Mazviita	Thank you
Doctor	Matest abuda. Ndineurombo kutaura izvi kuti mune HIV, uye mwana wenyu ane HIV zvakare. Nhau yakanaka ndeye kuti mishonga yeHIV inoshanda zvakanaka, inoku-batsira imi nemwanasikana	The test is back now. I am sorry to say that it shows that you and your child have HIV. The good news is that the medicines for HIV are very good now and they will help you and your child live long and healthy lives. It is much better

kuwedzera utano nemakore ekurarama. Zviri nani kuziva nezve HIV status yenyu uye kurapwa, pane kusaziva nekufa	to know your HIV status and treat it, than to not know and die.

Navigating an airport

Airports are often staffed by people who speak very good English. Nevertheless, addressing such beurocrats in good Shona may well keep them on your side in the event that rules are unexpectedly broken.

The situation: You are leaving Harare International Airport for Johannesburg and are standing in the queue to be processed by customs and immigration.

	Shona	**English**
Customs officer	Mumwe	Next
You	Mangwanani	Good morning
Customs officer	Ndipei passport yenyu	Please may I have your passport
You	Oyi	Here it is
Customs officer	Maiita basa re chii muZimbabwe?	What kind of work were you doing in Zimbabwe?
You	Ndaisevenzera MSF	I was working for MSF
Customs officer	Muchadzoka here?	Are you returning?
You	Ehe, ndichirikumirira work permit, saka ndichadzoka kana ndapiwa	Yes, I'm still waiting for my work permit, so I'll return when it's given to me

Customs officer	Mune madollar mangani?	How many dollars do you have?
You	Ndine $100 chete	I have $100 only
Customs officer	Mune zvamunoda kutiratidza here?	Do you have anything to declare?
You	Ndine macigarette 200	I have 200 cigarettes
Customs officer	Zvakanaka. Ndinoda kudhinda papassport. Endai	Very well. I want to stamp your passport. You may go.

Now we look at the situation of you re-entering the country and quibbling with a customs official over your visa.

	Shona	**English**
Customs officer	Mumwe	Next
You	Mangwanani	Good morning
Customs officer	Ndipei passport yenyu	Please may I have your passport
You	Oyi	Here it is
Customs officer	Wakapedzisira kushanya masvondo maviri akapera. Sei muchida kupinda zvakare?	You last finished visiting [ie you were last here] 2 weeks ago. Why do you want to enter again?
You	Ndichirikumirira visa re basa. Harisati rabuda.	I'm still waiting for my work visa, it hasn't yet come out [ie been issued].

Customs officer	Iyezvino, makapinda kakawanda. Handigoni kukupa visa. Munoda kusevenza muZimbabwe here?	Now you have entered too many times. I'm unable to give you a visa. Are you wanting to work in Zimbabwe?
You	Kana ndapiwa visa rebasa, ndichatanga kusevenza kuMSF. Asi iyezvino, ndichagara chete	When I receive my work permit I will start working at MSF. But now, I will just wait
Customs officer	Nhasi, ndichakupa visa. Asi, imwe nguva, hauchagona kupinda usina visa rebasa. Unoda mazuva mangani	Today I will give you a visa. But next time, you will not be able to enter without a work visa. How many days do you want
You	Ndipei 30	Please can I have 30
Customs officer	Zvinoita $70	That makes $70
You	Oyi	Here it is
Customs officer	Zvakanaka. Endai	Very well. You may go

Rural development

In this scenario you are an NGO worker overseeing a borehole being built for a rural school. The situation picks up after you have arrived at the school and greeted the school development team (SDT). You discuss with them where to situate the borehole and how to maintain it once it is operational.

	Shona	**English**
You	Ndiri pano nhasi neboka rangu rose: William, Fungisai neni. William achachera nzvimbo yekuisa	I am here today with my whole team, William, Fungisai and myself. William will dig the site

	borehole. Pashure, Fungisai achaisa mapipe ese panzvimbo ipapo. Pekupedzisira ndichataura nemi nezve ruchengetedzo	of the borehole. After, fungisai will lay the all the pipes in that site. Finally, I will talk to you about maintenance.
SDT	Nzvimbo yamakasarudza iri kupi?	Where is the proposed site?
You	Iri pakagomo padhuze nenandare yenhabvu	It's by the small hill close to the soccer pitch
SDT	Zvakanaka. Uchatanga kuchera rini?	Very well. When will you start drilling?
You	Pashure pemusangano nemi	After this meeting with you
SDT	Tichabatsira sei?	How should we help?
You	Panzvimbo iyoyo, Temai-temai zvese, uye bvisai matombo. Musabvumidza vana kutamba ikoko	At that site, please cut everything [ie plants, trees, grass] and remove all the rocks. Don't allow the children to play there.
SDT	Zvakanaka. Tinofanira kubhadara mari here?	Very well. Do we have to pay anything?
You	Kwete. NGO yedu ichabdhara.	No. Our NGO is paying.
SDT	Munotora nguva yakadii?	How much time will you take?
You	Tichapedza kuchera nhasi. Mangwana tichaisa mapipe uye tichataura nezve ruchengetedzo	We will finish drilling today. Tomorrow we'll lay the pipes and talk about maintenance
SDT	Zvakanaka. Ndiani achaita ruchengetedzo?	Very well. Who will do the maintenance?
You	Takawiririrana neSDT vhiki rakapera kuti ichasarudza munhu mumwe	We agreed with the SDT last week that it would choose a

	chete kudzidza kuchengetedza borehole. Boka redu richatanga kudzidzisa munhu uyu mangwana	single person to learn how to maintain the borehole. Our team will start training this person tomorrow.

We now return to you as you stand in front of the SDT and discuss user instructions and maintenance for the installed borehole.

	Shona	**English**
You	Kushandisa borehole iyi, munopomba se izvi. Munofanira kushandisa samba shoma. Edzai	To work this borehole you pump like this. You must use it gently. Please try.
Development team	Zvirinyore!	It's easy!
You	Ehe. Asi kuchengetedza kwakaoma. Ongororai vhiki roga roga. Kana borehole ratanga kunetsa, munofanira kutaura nemechanica watichadzidzisa nhasi	Yes. But maintenance is difficult. Please inspect it every week. If the borehole starts giving problems, you must speak to the mechanic that we will train today
Development team	Zvakanaka. Uchatanga kuchera rini?	Very well. When will you start drilling?
You	Pashure pemusangano nemi	After this meeting with you
Development team	Tichabatsira sei?	How should we help?

You	panzvimbo iyoyo, Temai-temai zvese, uye bvisai ma-tombo. Musabvumidza vana kutamba ikoko	At that site, please cut every-thing [ie plants, trees, grass] and remove all the rocks. Don't allow the children to play there.
Development team	Zvakanaka. Tinofanira kubhadara mari here?	Very well. Do we have to pay anything?
You	Kwete. NGO yedu ichabdhara.	No. Our NGO is paying.
Development team	Munotora nguva yakadii?	How much time will you take?
You	Tichapedza kuchera nhasi. Mangwana tichaisa mapipe uye tichataura nezve ruchengetedzo	We will finish drilling today. To-morrow we'll lay the pipes and talk about maintenance
Development team	Zvakanaka. Ndiani achaita ruchengetedzo?	Very well. Who will do the maintenance?
You	Takawiririrana nemi vhiki rakapera kuti muchasarudza munhu mumwe chete kudzidza kuchengetedza borehole. Boka richataura nemunhu uyu mangwana	We agreed with you last week that you would choose a single person to learn how to maintain the borehole. The team will talk to this person tomorrow.

Finally, you turn to the mechanic to be trained to maintain the borehole:

	Shona	English
You	Zuva roga roga. Ongororai mashandiro epumbi. Isai girizi panguva yakafanira. Ongororai manuts uye mabhaudi uye sunga panguva yakafanira. Pekupedzisira, ongororai fenzi uye gadzirisai maburi.	Daily. Inspect the workings of the pump. Put greese where necessary. Inspect the nuts and bolts and tighten where necessary. Finally, inspect the fence and fix holes.
Trainee	Zvakanaka.	Very well.
You	Pavhiki roga roga. Zorai girizi pamajoini, uye pose panofamba se izvi. Kupera kwemwedzi wega wega, ongororai huwandu hwemvura inobuda.	Every week. Put greese on the joints and everywhere that moves[77]. At the end of each month, inspect the quantity of water coming out.
Trainee	Ndinofanira kushandisa matool api?	Which tools must I use?
You	Shandisai matool aya. Tichamasiya pano nhasi.	Use these tools. We will leave them here today.
Trainee	Zvakanaka	How should we help?

[77]In other words, "on all moving parts".

Exercises

1. Translate the following dialogue between a carpenter and his contractor, into English:

Contractor Mangwanani. Nhasi tichabvisa pendi kubva pamagonhi matatu pamba. Pakupedza basa iro, torai mameasurement ese ekuvaka mashelf kukitchen.

Carpenter Zvakanaka. Kubvisa pendi munofanira kutenga paint-stripper, 3 litres. Zvinotora mazuva maviri kupedza basa iri. Kutanga basa kukitchen ndinoda mundiratidze kuti mashelf anoenda kupi. Ndinokumbirawo deposit nhasi kundotenga mapuranga.

Contractor Ndakatotenga paint-stripper kudhara, 5 litres. Saka munogona kuita magonhi ese nhasi. Kupedza mashelf ese, nekuisa varnish, zvese, imarii?

Carpenter Zvakanaka. Ndinoda 50% yevalue yemapuranga kuvaka mashelf. Sokuziva kwangu, kushandisa mapuranga epine, anoita $25/m. Saka tinofungidzira kuti tichashandisa 10m, saka pamwe chete, i-$250. Munobadhara 50%, saka $125 deposit.

Contractor Zvakanaka. Munoda kupiwa mari rudzii? Bond kana USD kana ma-Rand kana electronic transfer?

Carpenter Ini pachangu, ndinoda USD. Asi kuchitoro tinogona kushandisa card yenyu

Contractor Zvakanaka. Ndinoda kushandisa card nokuti USD inoshoma mazuva ano

Carpenter Zvakanaka. Ndichatanga iyezvino. Mune screpa here yekubvisa pendi?

Contractor Ehe. Tarisai mushedhi, unoiona pamadziro

2. Translate the following passage, concerning domestic work, from Shona into English.

You	Mangwanani Enereta. Nhasi gadzira spare room nokuti shamwari dzangu dziviri dzichauya vhiki rino. Waridza mubhedha, tsvaira pasi pose, pukuta mashelf uye mafafitera. Bvisa madandemutande mumakona ose.
Enereta	Zvakanaka. Asi cobra yakapera nezuro. Ndoita sei?
You	Ndichaenda nguva dzekumaranji kundoitenga
Enereta	Zvakanaka. Ndinofanira kuita sei iyezvino?
You	Ndinoda kuendesa marecycling-waste ese kuGreendale. Zvese zvirimukitcheni mucupboard pazasi pesingi. Zvinosanganisira maplastic, aluminium, nemabhodhoro. Isa mumabhegi matatu akasiyanasiyana, muchipatsanura maplastic, mabhodhoro ne aluminium
Enereta	Zvakanaka. Mabhegi anodiwa here kuiswa mutokari?
You	Ehe. Asi siya mabhodhoro mumba nokuti anorema zvakanyanya. Ndimirire, tichaita tese
Enereta	Kana ndapedza ndichaita chii?
You	Fanogeza bathroom ose neHandyandy netoilet cleaner uye isa matoilet roll matsva

3. Translate the following dialogue into Shona[78]. Where the Shona word isn't known (and doesn't exist in the dictionary component of this book) use an English word.

You	How can I help you?
Patient	My son has a running stomach
You	When did it start?
Mother	Three days ago
You	What did he eat?
Mother	He ate sadza and relish with the family only
You	And did he drink anything unusual
Mother	Yes, he drank water from a new well
You	Is this new well covered?
Mother	As far as I know, it isn't
You	I would like to test your son for typhoid. Does he have a temperature?
Mother	I don't know
You	I will take his temperature now then and give him some medicines to reduce the diarrhea
Mother	Very well

[78]The dialogue presented in this exercise is based on real experiences by doctors and nurses in Zimbabwe.

You	Your son must take these pills 3 times per day until completed. Come back tomorrow at 9am to collect your test results. Make sure that he washes his hands with soap after using the toilet
Mother	How much must I pay?
You	This medicine is free, but if the test shows typhoid, then you must pay a little
Mother	Okay, how much
You	Perhaps $2
Mother	Okay, I will return tomorrow.
You	If the diarrhea gets worse, bring him back later today
Mother	Thank you. I will do that

4. Translate the following passage into English, as best you can. What movie is the monologue below lifted from? [Hint: The movie stars Tom Cruise and Jack Nicholson]

Haugoni kutambira chokwadi! Mwanangu, tinorarama munyika ine miganhu inofanirwa kuchengetedzwa nevanhu vane pfuti. Ndiani achazviita? Iwe? Iwe, Lieutenant Weinberg? Ndine basa guru kupfura kunzwisisa kwako. Munochema nekuda kwaSantiago uye munozvidza Varwi. Mune rugare iroro. Mune rugare wekusaziva zvinhu zvandinoziva, kuti rufu rwaSantiago, rairwadza, asi rwakachengetedza hupenyu hwevanhu. Uye kuvapo kwangu kwauri kwakashata, haugoni kukunzwisisa, asi kunochengetedza hupenyu!

Haudi chokwadi, nokuti mukatikati memwoyo, hautauri nezve nyaya iyoyo pamafaro, munoda kuti ndinofanira kuva pamuganhu iwowo. Munondida pamuganhu iwowo. Tinoshandisa mazwi anoti "rukudzo", "hunhu", "ruvimbiko". Tinoshandisa mazwi aya sechitsigiro chehupenyu hwakapedzwa pakudzivirira chinhu. Munoashandisa sechisetso. Handina nguva kana handina chido kuzvitsanangura kumunhu anomuka uye kurara pasi pegumbezi ane rusununguko rwandinokupa, asi munhu anobvunza kuti ndinorupa sei. Ndingati zviri nani kungoti "mazviita", woenda. Pamwe, ndinoti nonga chombo, chengetedza nzvimbo. Kana kuti, handina hanya nezvaunofunga kuti ndozvaunofanirwa kuitwa.

Vocabulary:

-aina	iron
-bata	hold/catch
-batanidza	join
-bhara	wheel barrow
-bva pamuviri	miscarriage
-bvisa pamuviri	abortion
-bvumidza	permit [something to happen]
-bvunda	shake
-chaya	running stomach
-cheka	cut
-chenjera	beware of
-chera	dig/scoop
-dimbura	cut into pieces (like wires, brick, wood)
-dira	pour
-diridza	water/irrigate
-donza	pull
-dyara	plant seeds
-dzikisa	reduce
-dzikise	deepen
-dzivirira	protect
-dzura	pluck by hand
-dzvinya	press (button) or "hold tight"
-enzana	make level
-enzanisa	make level
-fema	breathe
-gadzira	fix/repair
-gumana	touch one another
-isa	put
-kanganwa	forget
-kiya – lock	lock
-kusvikira	reach

-kwesha	scrape/sand
-misa	stop/make steady
-moneredza	bind together by twisting (as with wire)
-mwaya	sprinkle
-nanikai	dry
-nonga	pick up
-ondoroka	lose weight
-patsanura	separate
-pera izwi	be hoarse
-pfeka	wear
-pfupikisa	shorten
-pomba	pump
-pukuta	wipe/clean
-putsa	knock down
-putsa	knock down
-rapwa	be healed
-rarama	survive/live
-ratidzika	to appear [as being something]
-rera vana	child spacing
-rodha	load
-rova	hit/hammer
-rutsa	vomit
-rwadzwa ne	to be in pain of [something, eg stomach]
-sada kudya	loss of appetite
-sakura	weed with an implement
-sanganisa	mix
-sarudza	choose
-sefa	sieve
-shanya	visit
-shaya hope	be sleepless
-shushikana	worry
-simudza	lift up
-simudza	lift/raise
-sunda	push
-sunga	tie/join
-sunungura	untie
-swatuka	straight
-takura	carry
-tambura	writhe with agony/anguish
-tiler	tile

-tsvaira	sweep
-tumbura	lance/spike
-turika	hang (often used when referring to roof sheets and scaffolding)
-unganidza	stack/pile
-vaka	build
-wacha	wash (in a washing machine or by hand)
-wedzera	increase or lift
-wirirana	agree with one another
-zora	apply [ointment/grease/etc]
-zora	apply (paint, cement)
-zvekusima	-transplant (plant material)
bakwa	wood pile
batanidza	join
bazi	branch (of a tree)
bhara	wheel barrow
bhaudi	bolt
boka	team
buri	hole
bvisa	remove
cheka	cut
chenjera	beware of
chera	dig/scoop
chidimbu	piece [of something]
chido	something wanted or desirable
chikosoro	nasal cough
chipfuva	chest cough
chisetso	something laughed at
chitsigiro	supporting structure
chombo	weapon
dama	cheek
dimbura	cut into pieces (like wires, brick, wood)
dira	pour
donza	pull
dumbu	stomach
dzinde	cutting [from a tree/shrub]
dzikisa	reduce
dzivirira pamuviri	birth control
dzungu	dizziness
dzvinya	press (button) or "hold tight"

futi	also
gadzira	make/build
girizi	grease
grass	uswa
hanya	care
hoe	badza
hove	fish
hunhu	code of conduct
huro	throat
huwandu	quantity
isa	put
ivhu	soil/sand
jekiseni	injection
kanzura	counsellor
kiyenura	unlock
kupisa muviri	run a temperature (when ill)
kushomeka kwemvura	deyhydration
kusvikira	reach
kuvapo kwangu	my existence
kwesha	scrape/sand
lintoro	lintel
mabhadi	bolts
mabonzo	bones
madandemutande	cobwebs
mafaro	entertainments
magetsi	electricity
maghirovisi	gloves
magirazi	spectacles
maiwe	expression of surprise or shock
majuru	termites
makonye	bacteria
manje manje	shortly (slang)
manyoka	diarrhoea
manyowa	manure
mapango	round poles
mapepa e basa	job contract
mapranga	planks of wood
marara	rubbish
mararia	malaria

maratta	roofing sheets
marimwezuro	day before yesterday
mashandiro	ways of doing things
masendipepa	sandpaper
mashandisiro	workings
mashizha	leaves
matadza	gums
mbabvu	rib
mbeu	seed
mechanica	mechanic
miganhu	borders
misa	stop, make steady
moneredza	bind together by twisting (as with wire)
mota	boil
muhomba – flower bed	flower bed
musana	back/spine
mushonga	medicine/chemicals
mwanasikana	daughter
mwaya	sprinkle
nandare yenhabvu	soccer pitch
nekuda kwa	because of [insert reason]
nepkeni	napkin
nhata	aphid
nhondo	seedling
nhunzi	fly
nzeve	ears
nzvimbo	place
onyeni	onion
pachipamwe	informal hello
pachipamwe	hi
pakupedzisira	finally or "to finish"
pfeka	wear
pfupikisa	shorten
pick	piki
pitsendi	pitsand
pukuta	wipe/clean
pump	pombi
putsa	knock down
rivasendi	riversand

ropa	blood
rova	hit/hammer
rufu	death
rugare	peace/luxury
rukudzo	respect
rurimi	tongue
rusununguko	freedom
ruvimbiko	loyalty
sanganisa	mix
sefa	sieve
semendi	cement
shuffle	foshoro
simudza	lift up
sora	weeds
sunda	push
sunga	tie/join
swatuka	straight (adjective)
tadza kuita weti	difficulty urinating
takura	carry
tambo dzemagetsi	electrical wires
tenga	buy
tsemuka	cracked (stative adjective)
tsvaira	sweep
turika	hang
urwa	puss
utachiwana	bacteria
utano	health
vaka	build
varwi	fighters
vavaki	builders
wedzera	increase or lift
zora	apply (paint, cement)
zvakajeka	it is clear
zvakakosha kuti	it's important [to do...]
zvidinha	bricks
zvipikiri	nails

APPENDIX

Answers

Lesson 1

1. For the following adjectives write down the adjective stem used.
    a. (example) muchero mudiki, Answer: **diki**
    b. (example) michero mikobvu. Answer: **kobvu**
    c. Huku guru (**kuru**)
    d. Mikaka mishoma (**shoma**)
    e. Shumba gobvu (**kobvu**)
    f. Vakomana varefu (**refu**)
    g. Mukadzi mutete (**tete**)

2. Fill in the correct prefix in the following sentences:
    a. Eg. mubiki **mu**pfupi
    b. Musikana **mu**refu
    c. Chibage **chi**tsvuku
    d. Mhuka **dzi**zhinji
    e. Badza dema (no prefix here either – no prefix for hard sounding words in their singular)
    f. Makomo **ma**tete

3. Place the correct pronoun in the following sentences for the stative adjective, "naka"
    a. Eg. Mukomana **waka**naka
    b. Mbudzi **ya**naka (singular)
    c. Michero **ya**naka
    d. Chingwa **chaka**naka
    e. Gomba **raka**naka
    f. Zviso **zvaka**naka
    g. Nguruve **dzaka**naka (plural)
    h. Makudo **aka**naka

4. Translate the following passage into English
    Rimwe zuva mukomana mudiki anorwara akaenda kuchipatara. Akati kunaDokota varefu , "ndine musoro".

Dokota vakabvunza kune mukomana, "wakatanga kurwadza rini?"

Mukomana akati, "wakatanga pandakadonha mugomba rakadzika."

Dokota akati, "ndinoda kuita X-ray, asi machine ye-X-ray yakafa. Saka, iyezvino ndichakupa mapiritsi akatsvuka 2."

One day a small sick boy went to the hospital. He said to the tall doctor, "I have a headache".

The doctor asked the boy, "when did it start?"

The boy said, "it started when I fell down in a deep hole."

The doctor said, "I would like to do an X-ray, but the the X-ray machine is broken. Therefore, now, I will give you two red pills."

Lesson 2

1. Choose the correct locative for the following sentences:
   a. Eg. Baba vakagara **pa**chigaro (pa/ku/mu)
   b. Mukomana achaenda **ku**chitoro (pa/ku/mu)
   c. Murume ari kubika **mu**mba (pa/ku/mu)
   d. Imbwa inorara **pa**nze (pa/ku/mu)
   e. Nhasi ndiri kunzwa **mu**dumbu (pa/ku/mu)
   f. Ndinobva **ku**France (pa/ku/mu)
   g. Tichatora vanhu **ku**chikoro (pa/ku/mu)
   h. **Pa**ne mukaka pashelf here? (pa/ku/mu)

2. Translate the following passage into English:
   Nezuro ndakanetswa nemapurisa kutaundi. Ndakazobhadhara $20 muripo kuchiteshi chemapurisa. Pashure pekubhadhara ndakazoenda kuNyanga. Ndakagara kuMontclair. Zuva iroro ndakaona makudo akawanda netsoko pagomo. Gudo rimwe chete rakapinda mumotokari. Ndakaridzinga asi rakaba mabanana angu pachigaro.

   Yesterday I was frustrated by the police in town. I eventually paid $20 as fine at the police station. After paying I finally went to Nyanga. I stayed at Montclaire. On that particular day I saw a lot of baboons and vervet monkeys on the rocks. One baboon entered the car. I chased it but it stole my bananas on the seat.

3. Translate the following into Shona:
   Every Monday I collect the children from school. After getting home they eat lunch in the kitchen and then afterwards play outside with their friends. When playing hide and seek they climb trees. Sometimes they fall and scrape their legs. Inside the house there are bandages to put on their wounds. At night they like to sleep near the television.

   Muvhuro wega wega ndinotora vana kuchikoro. Pakusvika kumba vanodya ranji mukicheni, pashure vanotamba panze neshamwari dzavo. Pakutamba chiwandewande vanokwira miti. Dzimwe nguva, vanodonha uye vanomarwa makumbo avo. Mukati memba mune mabhandeji kuisa pazvironda zvavo. Pausiku vanoda kurara pedyo nechivhitivhiti.

4. Translate the following into Shona:
    a. The rabbit is close to the road (Tsuro iri padhuze nemugwagwa)
    b. After some days, the car was stolen (mushure mamazuva motokari yakabiwa)
    c. The honey is on top of the table (huchi uri pamusoro petafura)
    d. The forest is beneath the mountain (sango iri pazasi pegomo)
    e. My work is far from home (basa rangu riri kure nemusha wangu)
    f. Is Tendai close to Susan? (Tendai ari pana Susan here?[80])
    g. Shingi is behind Tapiwa (Shingi ari pashure paTapiwa)
    h. Inside the cupboard you'll find the pliers (mukati mekabhati, uchawana mapliers)
    i. You are close to losing your money (uri pedyo nekurasa mari yako)

Lesson 3

1. Convert the following into the *past progressive* tense
    a. Vari kushandira kuMutare (vakanga vari kushandira kuMutare)
    b. Tiri kubikira chiremba chikafu (tanga tiri kubikira chiremba chikafu)
    c. Sadza ririkudyiwa neimbwa (sadza ranga riri kudyiwa neimbwa)

[80] "Tendai ari pedyo na Susan here?" would be equally valid, as would "Tendai ari padhuze naSusan here?"

d. Tii iri kumharwa nenhunzi (tii yakanga iri kumharwa nenhunzi)
e. Chitima chirikukwirwa nevanhu (chitima chaikwirwa nevanhu)
f. Movie irikufarirwa nevana (movie yaifarirwa nevana)
g. Ndiri kutaurira sekuru nezve birthday rangu (ndaitaurira sekuru nezve birthday rangu)

2. Convert the following sentences to their past tense:
   a. Ndine chitoro pedyo neZvishavane (ndakava nechitoro pedyo neZvishavane)
   b. Vana avo havana ruremekedzo nevakuru (vana avo havana kuva neruremekedzo nevakuru)
   c. Ndine mari yakawandisa (ndakava nemari yakawandisa)
   d. Hatina chikafu chose (hatina kuva nechikafu chose)
   e. Mombe inenyanga huru (mombe yaiva nenyanga huru)
   f. Zvipikiri zvine ngura (zvipikairi zvaiva nengura)
   g. Handina mhanza (handina kuva nemhanza)

3. Convert the following from the form "was" to the form "used to" with one of the time phrases (gore rakapera, vhiki rakapera, mwedzi wakapera, nezuro, muna 2000, mwaka wechando wakapera, muna nyamavhuvhu, pakati peusiku, gore roga roga) and a location of your choice.
   a. Eg. Taibika tese
      Gore rakapera, taibika tese kumba kwaMai
   b. Nyati dzaidya uswa (mwedzi wakapera, nyati dzaidya uswa mumunda)
   c. Mvura yainaya (muna 2000, mvura yainaya kuChiredzi)
   d. Mashizha aibhururutswa (muna nyamavhuvhu, mashizha aibhururutswa mudenga)

e. Vanababa vaigadzira pombi (pakati peusiku, vanababa vaigadzira pombi kuchiteshi chemafuta)
f. Jongwe raikukuridza (vhiki rakapera, jongwe raikukuridza panze)
g. Mbavha yaiba upfu (nezuro, mbavha yaiba upfu mukicheni)
h. Mapurisa aimisa midhudhudhu (mwaka wechando wakapera, mapurisa aimisa midhudhudhu kuGweru)
i. Amai vaitumira tsamba (gore roga roga, amai vaitumira tsamba kumusha)

4. Translate the following conditional tense sentences into English:
   a. Ndingadai ndichigadzira motokari dai ndine zvipanera (I would fix the motorcar if only I had spanners)
   b. Tingadai tichisimudza mapango dai tine tambo (We would raise the planks if only we had rope)
   c. Tingadai tichihwanda mvura, dai tine tendi (we would hide from the rain, if only we had a tent)
   d. Vangadai vachishandira pamba dai vane wifi (they would work at home if only they had wifi)
   e. Huni dzingadai dzakagara dai tine magetsi (the wood would have remained if only we'd had electricity)
   f. Zvipatara zvingadai zvakavhura dai zvine mushonga (the hospitals would have opened if only they'd had medicine)
   g. Sadza ringadai rakadyiwa dai rine muriwo (the sadza would have been eaten if only it had had relish [with it])

Lesson 4

1. Convert the following passive sentences to their active form
    a. Eg. Miriwo iri kugezwa nemubiki
       Mubiki ari kugeza miriwo
    b. Gumbo rangu rakakuvadzwa nebhodhoro (bhodhoro rakakuvadza gumbo rangu)
    c. Ndiri kunetswa nemotokari yangu (motokari yangu iri kundinetsa)
    d. Sadza richapedziswa nemakonzo (makonzo achapedzisa sadza)
    e. Mugwagwa wakagadziriswa nekanzuru (kanzuru yakagadzirisa mugwagwa)
    f. Vakashandiswa naboss wavo (boss wavo vakavashandisa)
    g. Kitsi dzinodaidzwa naChipo (Chipo anodaidza kitsi)
    h. Tichanyorerwa nezve madate ematesti nemudzidzisi wedu (mudzidzisi wedu achatinyorera nezve madate ematesti)

2. Convert the following passage into its passive form, where possible.

   Mazuva ose chiremba vanoongorora murwere. Chiremba vanopa murwere mapiritsi. Masikati chiremba vanobaya jekiseni murwere uye manheru chiremba vanonyorera murwere prescription. Pashure chiremba vanotsanangurira murwere nezve kushandisa mapiritsi nguva dzose. Pashure, murwere anotenda chiremba.

   Mazuva ose murwere anoongororwa naChiremba. Murwere anopiwa mapiritsi naChiremba. Masikati murwere anobayiwa jekseni naChiremba uye manheru murwere anonyorerwa prescription naChiremba. Pashure, murwere anotsanangurirwa nezve kushandiswa kwemapiritsi nguva dzose naChiremba. Pashure, chiremba anotendwa nemurwere.

Lesson 5

1. Extend the following verbs with *ira/era*:
    a. Eg. Fara
    b. Geza - gezera
    c. Bika - bikira
    d. Gara - garira
    e. Simudza - simudzira
    f. Punza - punzira
    g. Pwanya - pwanyira
    h. Dzvinya - dzvinyira
    i. Potsa – potsera

2. Extend the verbs in question 1, above, with *isa*.
    a. Eg. Fara - farisa
    b. Geza - gezesa
    c. Bika - bikisa
    d. Gara - garisa
    e. Simudza - simudzisa
    f. Punza - punzisa
    g. Pwanya - pwanyisa
    h. Dzvinya – dzvinyisa
    i. Potsa - potsesa

3. Translate the following sentences into English:
    a. Eg. Mazuva ose mukomana anotumira zvidhina kuvaka imba (Every day the boy sends bricks [in order] to build the house)
    b. Mazuva ose mukomana anotumira zvidhina John (Every day the boy sends bricks to John)
    c. Vabereki vachanyorera tsamba vana (The parents will write letters to the children)

d. Ndine mhanza nekubatsirwa kutora driver's license naJohn (I am lucky to be helped to get a driver's license by John)
e. Tinoda kutengerwa mapiritsi kuchitoro (We want to have pills bought [for us] at the store)
f. Chimbuzi chirikugadzirwa kuzoshandiswa kumutambo (The toilet is being fixed in order be used during the party)
g. Mapango akavezerwa kuvaka chimufananidzo (The planks were carved for the purposing of constructing a statue)
h. Vaitaurira Shephard nezve mapurisa (They used to speak to Shephard about the police)

4. Translate the following into English:
    a. Tiri kushandiswa nemabhengi kubvuma mabondi (Eg. We are being used by the banks through [our] acceptance of bond notes)
    b. Mhanyisa kundotengesa[81] fodya kuchitoro (run fast to sell tobacco at the store)
    c. Sungisa mapango newaya (tile the poles with the wire)
    d. Simudzisa lintel netambo (lift the lintel with the rope)
    e. Tangisa sendenzi nevara guru (Start the sentence with a capital letter)
    f. KuSouth Africa kune zvinhu zvaunoda zvakawandisa (in South Africa there are a lot of things that you like)
    g. Musawanzisa shuga mucoffee yangu (don't put a lot of sugar in my coffee)
    h. Madomasi ari kukurisa gore rino nemvura yakawandisa (the tomatoes are growing fast this year with a lot of water)

[81]Note that "ku ndo[verb]" in this sentence means "for the purpose of" and therefore conveys the same meaning as a verb extended with "ira". In this particular example, it would have been just as accurate to say, "mhanyisira kutengesa fodya kuchitoro".

Lesson 6

1. Translate the following into Shona, using mbo, to, ndo, zo, fumo, wanzo, where necessary:
    a. Eg. I have never gone to South Africa (Handina ku**mbo**enda kuSouth Africa)
    b. I once saw a leopard (Ndaka**mbo**ona mbada)
    c. Have you returned the scissors already? (Maka**to**dzosera zvigero here?)
    d. He helped to fix the car and then, finally, drove home (Akabatsira kugadzira motokari aka**zo**tyaira kumba)
    e. I ran to the store early in the morning in order to buy milk, but saw that ther store was already closed (Nda**fumo**mhanya kuchitoro ku**ndo**tenga mukaka, asi ndaona kuti chitoro cha**to**vharwa)
    f. In my heart of hearts I already know the truth (Mukatikati memwoyo wangu ndinoziva chokwadi)
    g. At work I frequently embarrass[82] myself by arriving late (Kubasa ndinowanzo kuzvinyadzisa nekunonoka kusvika)
    h. The rat ate all the food but, after some days, it finally died of starvation (Gonzo rakadya chikafu chose, asi mushure mamazuva, yak**zo**afa nenzara)
    i. They worked in order to save for a good holiday (Vakashanda ku**ndo**chengetedza mari yezororo rakanaka)
    j. Have you ever met a person with a good heart like that? (Maka**mbo**sangana munhu ane mwoyo wakanaka zvakadaro here?)
    k. I thought that you had already found a job you like (Ndaifunga kuti waka**to**wana basa raunoda)

[82]Note that you will need to use a reflexive here!

2. Translate the following passage into English:

   Gore roga roga ndaiwanzoenda kuzororo kuNyanga kupurazi kweshamwari yangu kundomubatsira nebasa. Panguva iyoyo ndaifumomuka kundochengetedza zvipfuyo. Ndaisevenza chaizvo kuzvitarisa, asi rimwe zuva imwe mbudzana yakatanga mhanya-mhanya kwese kwese. Ndakaedza kuidzora asi ndakatadza. Mbudzana yakazorasika. Handina kumboiona zvakare.

   Each and every year I always used to go on holiday to Nyanga to my friend's farm in order to help him with work. At that particular time I used to wake up very early in order to look after the livestock. I used to work a lot at watching them, but one day a kid started running all over the place. I tried to shepherd it [back to the group] but I failed. The kid finally got lost. I never saw it again.

Lesson 7

1. For the following sentences, choose whether to use "ne", "na" or "neku".
   a. Eg. Taienda **na**Tendai kundochera mvura
      We used to go **with** Tendai to collect water
   b. Hapana anoziva kuti Jim **ne**shamwari yake vaenda kupi
   c. Chipembere chichanwa mvura **ne**dzimwe mhou kurwizi
   d. Pazororo tichafamba kuTriangle **neku**Chimanimani
   e. Vakaendeswa **na**chiremba kuchipatara **neku**pharmacy
   f. Pakusvika kuNgomakurira **neku**Domboshava, Trevor **na**Farai vakadzinga makudo **ne**tsoko
   g. Tichavhara maburi **neku**isa putty mukati
   h. Nyoka dzakapinda mumba **neku**kwira madziro
2. Translate the following into Shona, paying attention to the use of "nokuti" and "pamusoro pe" when translating "because", "on account of", or "through".

a. I succeeded at the exam **because** I studied (Eg. Ndakabudirira bvunzo **nokuti** ndakaverenga)
b. Everyone knows the truth **because** they speak to experts (Vanhu vose vanoziva chokwadi **nokuti** vanotaura nenyanzvi)
c. The plane crashed **because** the engines failed (Ndege yakarovera pasi **nokuti** maengines akafa)
d. The economy failed **because** of bond notes (Hupfumi hwakakundikana **pamusoro pe**mabond-note)
e. The dogs survived the winter **on account of** finding food (Imbwa dzakararama panguva yechando **pamusoro pe**kuwana chikafu)
f. The policeman found the thief **through** examining some footprints (Mupurisa akawana mbava **pamusoro pe**kuongorora matsimba)
g. Motocars can break down **on account of** poor maintenance (Motokari dzinogona kufa **pamusoro pe**kutadza kuchengetedza zvakanaka)
h. They are going on holiday **because** they found enough money (Vari kuenda kuzororo **nokuti** vakawana mari yakakwana)

3. Translate the following passage into English (with special emphasis on thinking about "sezvo", "kana", "kana hazvo", "asi" and "nyango"):

Pandaisevenza kuGokwe ndaiziva mumwe mukadzi aiva nemwoyo wakanaka **nyango** aiva nehupenyu hwakaoma. **Sekuti**, rimwe zuva ndakaona mukadzi uyu akabatsira mukomana akanga asina chinhu chose. **Panguva iyoyo** ndaiona kuti vanhu vese vakanga vari mumatambudziko ikoko kuGokwe. Nguva dzose ndaishamisika kuti sei mukadzi uyu aiva nemwoyo wakachena. Takapesana **sezvo** ndaifanira kudzoka kuHarare **kana hazvo** ndaida kugara ikoko. (When I used to work in Gokwe I used to know a woman who had a good heart, **despite** having a difficult life. **For example**, one day I saw this woman help a boy who was without anything at all. **At that time** I used to observe that everyone was in difficulty in Gokwe. All the time I was astonished by how this woman [could have] a kind heart. We parted from each other **since** I had to return to Harare, **although** I had wanted to stay there.)

4. Translate the following into Shona (with special emphasis on using "hence"/ "therefore"):
   a. The workers help each other and, hence, the business works well (Vasevenzi vanobatsirana **nekudaro** basa rinofamba zvakanaka)
   b. The teachers know how to teach, therefore, their students know a lot (Vadzidzisi vanoziva kudzidzisa nekudaro vadzidzi vanoziva chaizvo)
   c. The car hit the pothole and, henceforth, crashed into the lorry (Motokari yakapinda mupothole **nekudaro** yakarovera rori)
   d. Hungry leopards look for food on farms and, as such, kill many goats (Mbada dzine nzara dzinotsvaga chikafu mumapurazi nekudaro, dzinouraya mbudzi dzakawanda)
   e. The journalist will ask probing questions and, henceforth, get into trouble (Mutapi wenhau achabvunza mibvunzo nekudaro achapinda mumatambudziko)
   f. When repairing the car, you will see where the hole is and, therefore, know where to put the putty (Pakugadzira motokari, uchaona kuti buri iri kupi nekudaro, uchaziva kuti unofanira kuisa putty kupi)

g. Those particular doctors have no medicines and, as such, are unable to help their patients (Vanachiremba ivavo havana mishonga nekudaro, havagoni kubatsira varwere)
h. The bond notes have entered the market and, as such, have caused inflation (Mabondnotes akapinda mumarket, **nekudaro**, akakonzera inflation)

Lesson 8

1. Convert the following verbs into their reciprocal form and use them in a sentence:
   a. Ona
      Eg. Tichaona**na** mangwana kuchikoro
   b. Dzidzisa
      Tichadzidzisana mathematics
      (We will teach each other mathematics)
   c. Tuka
      Vakatukana kuti ndiani achatanga kuputa fodya
      (They verbally attacked each other over who would get to smoke the cigarrtte first)
   d. Seka
      Vaisekana panguva iyoyo nokuti vaitadza kunyora izwi yekuti "mbada"
      (They used to laugh at each other at that time because they would fail to spell the word "leopard")
   e. Takura
      Takatakurana nokuti takanga taneta
      (We carried each other because we were tired)
   f. -pa
      Vachapana rubatsiro
      (They will give each other assistance)
   g. Dhuma

Motokari dzakadhumana nokuti dzakanga dzisina magetsi (The motocars crashed into each other because they were without lights)

h. Guma
Makudo akagumana nokuti akanga arimapofu
(The baboons bumped heads because they were blind)

2. Translate the following sentences into Shona:
    a. I will cook sadza for **myself** at the house (Ndicha**zvi**bikira sadza pacha**ngu** kumba)
    b. You will buy **yourself** clothes at the end of the month (Ucha**zvi**tengera mbatya kupera kumwedzi)
    c. He drove the car to the store by **himself** (Aka**zvi**tyairira motokari kuchitoro)
    d. They fixed the toilet by **themselves** (Vaka**zvi**gadzirira chimbuzi)
    e. They sometimes wash **themselves** in the river (Dzimwe nguva vano**zvi**gezera murwizi)
    f. On returning to the mountain, he roasted the rabbit for **himself** (Pakudzokera kugomo, aka**zvi**gochera tsuro)
    g. When we see elephants we kill **ourselves** running[83] (Kana tichiona nzou tino**zvi**uraya nekumhanya)
    h. She was full of praise for **herself** (Akazadzwa neku**zvi**rumbidza)
    i. When cutting the vegetables he accidentally cut **himself** (Pakucheka miriwo aka**zvi**cheka)

3. Translate the following sentences into English:

[83]Note that there is an expression in Shona for "killing yourself" by doing some activity. In this case "killing yourself running" is an expression, similar to what you might find in English, emphasizing the rigour with which the running is being carried out.

a. Aramba kundipa makeys (She refused to give me the keys)
b. Ndicharamba kuenda ikoko (I will refuse to go over there)
c. Vanoramba kuteerera mudzidzisi (They refuse to listen to the teacher)
d. Munoramba muchifamba kusvikira pa"Giveway" (Continue walking until the "Giveway" sign)
e. Ndicharamba ndichinamatira kupora kwemunin'ina wangu (I will keep on praying for my younger brother to heal)
f. Ndinomuda asi anoramba achindiramba (I love her but she persists in refusing me)
g. Pakupedza kuverenga bhuku iro, ndicharamba kuriverenga zvakare (On finishing reading that book, I will refuse to read it again)
h. Vakanga varikuramba kukwira bhazi (They were refusing to board the bus)
i. Vakanga vachingoramba vachiverenga bepanhau kudzidza nezve nyaya dzehupfumi (They were persistent in reading the newspaper to learn about economics)
j. Vakaramba vachitsvaga bepanhau (They persisted looking for the newspaper)

4. Translate the following into Shona using either "kupfura" or "pane":
   a. I like that car more than the other one (Ndinoda motokari iyo **kupfura** motokari iyo)
   b. I like this person more than that one (Ndinoda munhu uyu pane uyo)
   c. There are more trees here than in South Africa (Kune miti mizhinji kuno pane kuSouth Africa)
   d. Our economy is smaller nowadays than long ago (Hupfumi hwedu hudiki mazuva ano pane kare)

e. Tall people are more likely to get cancer than short people (Vanhu varefu vangangogona kubatwa necancer pane vanhu vapfupi)
f. This carving is more beautiful than that one (Chivezwa ichi chakanaka pane icho)
g. My life is better now than it was last year (Hupenyu hwangu hwakanaka iyezvino pane gore rakapera)
h. These dresses are more expensive here than in town (Marokwe aya anodhura pano pane kutaundi)

5. Translate the following into Shona using "like this" or "like that" where necessary:
   a. Remove the rotten areas from the vegetables with the knife, **like this** (Eg. Bvisai nzvimbo dzakaora pamiriwo ne-banga, **se izvi**)
   b. As far as I'm told, you examine the stomach of the patient using the stethoscope, like this (Sokuudzwa kwangu, munoongorora mudumbu memurwere muchishandisa stethoscope se izvi)
   c. Mix the eggs with the oil, like that (Sanganisai mazai nemafuta, se izvo)
   d. Cut the wire with the pliers, like that (Cheka waya nepinjisi, se izvo)
   e. Put the potatoes and the butternut into the oven, like this (Isai mapotato nebutternut muoveni, se izvi)
   f. Lift the lintel onto the wall, like that (Simudzai lintel pa-madziro, se izvo)
   g. Spray the seedlings with chemicals, like this (Mwayai nhondo mushonga, se izvi)
   h. As far as I know, you attach the rope to the pole, like this (Sokuziva kwangu, munosunga tambo pabango, se izvi)

6. Translate the following into Shona, with special reference to using what you learned about "like him/her/them etc":
   a. She is beautiful like you (Eg. Akanaka **sewe**)
   b. You are a liar, like her (Uri munyepi, saiye)
   c. They sometimes fail to fulfill their dreams, like us (Dzimwe nguva vanotadza kuzadzisa zviroto, sesu)
   d. On the one hand, I drive to work early, like him, but on the other, I always arrive late, like him (Kune rimwe divi, Ndinofumotyaira kubasa, saiye, asi kune rimwe divi, ndinonoka kusvika saiye)
   e. They drink a lot, like us (Vanonwa doro chaizvo, sesu)
   f. You sing very well, like them (Unoimba zvakanaka chaizvo, savo)
   g. I like to win, like you (Ndinoda kukunda, sewe)
   h. They like to eat at restaurants, like us (Vanoda kudya kumarestaurant, sesu)

7. Make the following verbs into nouns using (mu/va or chi/zvi) and translate them into English:
   a. Eg. -nyora (va)
      Vanyori (writers)
   b. -nyoresa (zvi)
      zvinyoreso (pens)
   c. -shamisa (chi)
      chishamiso (a surprising thing)
   d. -tyaira (mu)
      mutyairi (driver)
   e. -tema (mu)
      mutemi (a tree feller)
   f. -tuwina (va)
      vatuwini (swimmers)

g. -kwira (va)
vakwiri (climbers)
h. -bika (zvi)
zvibiko (cooked foods)
i. -veza (chi)
chivezwa (something carved, ie carving)

Lesson 9

1. Translate the following sentences into Shona:
    a. The woman doesn't pay taxes and, therefore, is **playing with fire** (Mukadzi habhadari matexes, saka **ari kutamba nemoto**)
    b. On seeing the hyena we ran as fast as our legs could carry us (Pakuona bere takamhanya k**ubereka gotsi**)
    c. I left that woman because she isn't trustworthy (Ndakasiya mukudzi uyo nokuti anoita **gumbo mumba, gumbo panze**)
    d. I'm angry with my friend because he's got a big mouth (Ndine hasha neshamwari yangu nokuti ane muromo mukuru)
    e. I tried to beat him but I eventually threw the towel in (Ndakaedza kumukunda asi ndakazo**kanda mapfumo pasi**)
    f. She often asked for money because she had no shame (Aiwanzobvunza nezve mari nokuti ha**ana ganda kumeso**)
    g. I went to see grandmother last month, and she was hanging on to life by a thread (Ndakaenda kundoona mbuya mwedzi wakapera, **vaiva hari yofanzirofa**)
    h. Fixing the radiator when the engine is broken is a pointless waste of time (Kugadzira radiator kana engine yafa ari ku**dzingirira mhepo**)

2. Finish off the following common idioms and proverbs
    a. Ane ganda ane nyama **hazvienzani neasina**
    b. Kunhongwa **neatanga**
    c. Moyo, muti unomera **paunoda**
    d. Gumbo mumba, **gumbo panze**
    e. **kutamba** nemoto
    f. **Nyamunatsi** ndiye nyakubayiwa
    g. **Aiva madziva** ava mazambuko
    h. Mbada isati yadya vana vayo inotanga **yavapomera kuti vanonhuwa kunge mbudzi**

Lesson 10

1. Translate the following dialogue between a carpenter and his contractor, into English:

Contractor Mangwanani. Nhasi tichabvisa pendi kubva pamagonhi matatu pamba. Pakupedza basa iro, torai mameasurement ese ekuvaka mashelf kukitchen.

Good morning. Today we will remove paint from three doors in the house. On finishing that work, take all the measurements to build the shelves in the kitchen.

Carpenter Zvakanaka. Kubvisa pendi munofanira kutenga paint-stripper, 3 litres. Zvinotora mazuva maviri kupedza basa iri. Kutanga basa kukitchen ndinoda mundiratidze kuti mashelf anoenda kupi. Ndinokumbirawo deposit nhasi kundotenga mapuranga.

Very well. To remove the paint you must buy paint-stripper, 3 litres. It takes 3 days to finish this work. To start the work in the kitchen I'd like you to show me where the shelves go. I also ask for a deposit today to buy the planks.

Contractor Ndakatotenga paint-stripper kudhara, 5 litres. Saka munogona kuita magonhi ese nhasi. Kupedza mashelf ese, nekuisa varnish, zvese, imarii?

I already bought the paint-stripper a while ago, 5 litres. As such, you're able to do all the doors today. On finishing all the shelves, and applying varnish, on all of them, how much will it be?

Carpenter Zvakanaka. Ndinoda 50% yevalue yemapuranga kuvaka mashelf. Sokuziva kwangu, kushandisa mapuranga epine, anoita $25/m. Saka tinofungidzira kuti tichashandisa 10m, saka pamwe chete, i-$250. Munobadhara 50%, saka $125 deposit.

Very well. I'd like 50% of the value of the planks to build the shelf. As far as I know, to use pine planks, it's $25/m. Therefore, we guess that we'll buy 10m - total, it makes $250. You [should] pay 50%, therefore $125 deposit.

Contractor Zvakanaka. Munoda kupiwa mari rudzii? Bond kana USD kana maRand kana electronic transfer?

Very well. What kind of money would you like to be given? Bond, USD, Rands, or electronic transfer?

Carpenter Ini pachangu, ndinoda USD. Asi kuchitoro tinogona kushandisa card yenyu

Myself, I prefer USD. But at the store we can use your card.

Contractor Zvakanaka. Ndinoda kushandisa card nokuti USD inoshoma ma-zuva ano

Very well. I would like to use my card because USD are scarce these days.

Carpenter Zvakanaka. Ndichatanga iyezvino. Mune screpa here yekubvisa pendi?

Good. I will start now. Do you have a scraper for removing the paint.

Contractor Ehe. Tarisai mushedhi, unoiona pamadziro

Yes. Look in the shed, you will see it on the wall

2. Translate the following passage, concerning domestic work, from Shona into English.

You Mangwanani Enereta. Nhasi gadzira spare room nokuti shamwari dzangu dziviri dzichauya vhiki rino. Waridza mubhedha, tsvaira pasi pose, pukuta mashelf uye mafafitera. Bvisa madandemutande mumakona ose.

Good morning Enereta. Today tidy the spare room because two friends of mine will come this week. Make up the beds, sweep everywhere, clean the shelves and the windows. Remove the cobwebs from all the corners.

Enereta Zvakanaka. Asi Cobra yakapera nezuro. Ndoita sei?

Very well. But the Cobra finished yesterday. What should I do?

You Ndichaenda nguva dzekumaranji kundoitenga

I will go at lunch time to buy it

Enereta Zvakanaka. Ndinofanira kuita sei iyezvino?

Good. What should I do now?

You Ndinoda kuendesa marecycling-waste ese kuGreendale. Zvese zvirimukitcheni mucupboard pazasi pesingi. Zvinosanganisira maplastic, aluminium, nemabhodhoro. Isa mumabhegi matatu akasiyanasiyana, muchipatsanura maplastic, mabhodhoro ne aluminium

I would like to send all the recyling waste to Greendale. Everything that's in the kitchen in the coupboard beneath the sink. Including plastics, alumnium, bottles. Put them in 3 different bags, separating plastics, bottles and aluminium

Enereta Zvakanaka. Mabhegi anodiwa here kuiswa mutokari?

Fine. Should the bags be put in the car?

You Ehe. Asi siya mabhodhoro mumba nokuti anorema zvakanyanya. Ndimirire, tichaita tese

Yes. But leave the bottles inside because they're very heavy. Wait for me, we'll do it together.

Enereta Kana ndapedza ndichaita chii?

When I finish, what should I do?

You Fanogeza bathroom ose neHandyandy netoilet cleaner uye isa matoilet roll matsva

Do all the bathrooms with Handyandy and toilet cleaner and put new toilet rolls [out]

3. Translate the following dialogue into Shona[84]. Where the Shona word isn't known (and doesn't exist in the dictionary component of this book) use an English word.

You How can I help you?

Ndingakubatsirai sei?

[84]The dialogue presented in this exercise is based on real experiences by doctors and nurses in Zimbabwe

Patient	My son has a running stomach
	Mukomana wangu ane manyoka
You	When did it start?
	Akatanga rini?
Mother	Three days ago
	Mazuva matatu akapera
You	What did he eat?
	Akadya chii?
Mother	He ate sadza and relish with the family only
	Akadya sadza nerelish nemhuri chete
You	And did he drink anything unusual?
	Akanwa zvaasingagaronwi here?
Mother	Yes, he drank water from a new well
	Ehe, akanwa mvura kubva kutsime itsva
You	Is this new well covered?
	Tsime itsva yakavaridzirwa here?
Mother	As far as I know, it isn't
	Sokuziva kwangu, kwete
You	I would like to test your son for typhoid. Does he have a temperature?
	Ndinoda kumupa test yetyphoid. Ane temperature here?

Mother I don't know

Handizivi

You I will take his temperature now then and give him some medicines to reduce the diarrhea

Ndichatora temperature yake iyezvino uye ndichamupa mishonga pamusoro pekudzikisa temperature

Mother Very well

Zvakanaka

You Your son must take these pills 3 times per day until completed. Come back tomorrow at 9am to collect your test results. Make sure that he washes his hands with soap after using the toilet

Mukomana wenyu anofanira kutora mapiritsi matatu zuva rega rega kusvika pakupedza. Dzokera zvakare mangwana kuma 9am kuzotora maresult enyu. Ivai nechokwadi kuti anogeza maoko nesipho mushure mekushandisa chimbuzi

Mother How much must I pay?

Ndinofanira kubadhara madora mangani?

You This medicine is free, but if the test shows typhoid, then you must pay a little

Mushonga uyu mahara, asi kana une typhoid, unobhadhara mari shoma

Mother Okay, how much

Zvakanaka, imarii?

You	Perhaps $2
	Pamwe $2
Mother	Okay, I will return tomorrow
	Zvakanaka, ndichadzoka zvakare mangwana
You	If the diarrhea gets worse, bring him back later today
	Kana manyoka awedzera, munogona kudzoka naye
Mother	Thank you. I will do that
	Mazviita. Ndichaita

4. Translate the following passage into English, as best you can. What movie is the monologue below lifted from? [Hint: The movie stars Tom Cruise and Jack Nicholson]

Haugoni kutambira chokwadi! Mwanangu, tinorarama munyika ine miganhu inofanirwa kuchengetedzwa ne vanhu vane pfuti. Ndiani achazviita? Iwe? Iwe, Lieutenant Weinberg? Ndine basa guru kupfura kunzwisisa kwako. Munochema nekuda kwaSantiago uye munozvidza varwi. Mune rugare iroro. Mune rugare wekusaziva zvinhu zvandinoziva, kuti rufu rwaSantiago, rairwadza, asi rwakachengetedza hupenyu hwevanhu. Uye kuvapo kwangu kwauri kwakashata, haugoni kukunzwisisa, asi kunochengetedza hupenyu!

Haudi chokwadi, nokuti mukatikati memwoyo, hautauri nezve nyaya iyoyo pamafaro, munoda kuti ndinofanira kuva pamuganhu iwowo. Munondida pamuganhu iwowo. Tinoshandisa mazwi anoti "rukudzo", "hunhu", "ru-vimbiko". Tinoshandisa mazwi aya sechitsigiro chehupenyu hwakapedzwa pakudzivirira chinhu. Munoashandisa sechisetso. Handina nguva kana handina chido kuzvitsanangura kumunhu anomuka uye kurara pasi pegumbezi ane rusununguko rwandinokupa, asi munhu anobvunza kuti ndinorupa sei. Ndingati zviri nani kungoti "mazviita", woenda. Pamwe, ndinoti nonga chombo, chengetedza nzvimbo. Kana kuti, handina hanya nezva unofunga kuti ndozvaunofanirwa kuitwa.

Movie: A few good men. Scene: The "you can't handle the truth!" moment in which colonel Jessop becomes riled to the extent that (in the proceeding scene, not here shown) he admits, in a moment of anger, his culpability in the death of private Santiago. The original English from colonel Jessop is as follows:

You can't handle the truth! Son, we live in a world that has walls. And those walls have to be guarded by men with guns. Who's gonna do it? You? You, Lt. Weinberg? I have a greater responsibility than you can possibly fathom. You weep for Santiago and you curse the marines. You have that luxury. You have the luxury of not knowing what I know: that Santiago's death, while tragic, probably saved lives. And my existence, while grotesque and incomprehensible to you, saves lives...You don't want the truth. Because deep down, in places you don't talk about at parties, you want me on that wall. You need me on that wall.

We use words like honor, code, loyalty...we use these words as the backbone to a life spent defending something. You use 'em as a punchline. I have neither the time nor the inclination to explain myself to a man who rises and sleeps under the blanket of the very freedom I provide, then questions the manner in which I provide it! I'd rather you just said thank you and went on your way. Otherwise, I suggest you pick up a weapon and stand a post. Either way, I don't give a damn what you think you're entitled to!

DICTIONARY

Dictionary

SHONA – ENGLISH

-aina	iron
-ba	steal
-badhara	pay
-bata	hold/catch
-batana	work with each other
-batsira	help
-batsirana	help each other
-bayiwa	get stabbed
-bhururuka	fly
-bika	cook
-biwa	stolen
-budirira	succeed
-bva pamuviri	miscarriage
-bvisa pamuviri	abortion
-bvuma	accept
-bvumidza	permit [something to happen]
-bvunda	shake
-chaya	running stomach
-cheka	punzwa
-chekwa	broken
-chema	cry
-chengetedza	keep/look after
-daidza	call
-dhuma	bump
-dhumana	bump into each other
-dhumana	crash into each other
-diridza	water/irrigate
-donha	fall
-donza	pull
-donza	pull
-draiva	drive
-dumira	crash into
-dyara	plant seeds
-dzidza	learn
-dzidzisa	teach
-dzidzisana	teach each other
-dzika	reduce

-dzikira	– to reduce/shrink
-dzikise	deepen
-dzimura	extinguish [fire]
-dzinga	chase
-dzingirira	chase
-dzipwa	be choked
-dzivirira	protect
-dzora	shepherd [back somewhere]
-dzosera	return [something]
-dzura	pluck by hand
-dzvinya	press
-enda	go
-enzana	make level
-expaya	expire
-fema	breathe
-funga	think/miss
-fungana	miss each other
-gera	shave
-geza	wash
-gezana	wash each other
-gotcha	braai/barbecue/roast
-gumana	touch one another
-gutsa	feed
-itirana	do [to] each other
-kakama	stutter
-kakavadzana	argue with one another
-kanda	throw
-kanganwa	forget
-kiya – lock	lock
-konzera	cause
-konzeresa	cause
-kora	thick
-kudza	to respect
-kudzana	to respect each other
-kundikana	fall
-kundikana	fail
-kura	grow
-kuvadzwa	injured by
-kwana	enough
-kwira	climb

-marwa	scrape
-mera	grow/germinate
-mhanya-mhanya	rush
-mhara	land
-mhoresa	greet
-mhoresana	greet each other
-misa	stop
-naka	good
-nakidza	interest
-namata	pray
-nanikai	dry
-netsa	bother
-netsana	bother each other
-netswa	bothered by
-ngwara	clever (used statively)
-nhongwa	be picked
-nhuwa	smell [like something]
-nonga	pick up
-nyadzisa	embarress
-nyora	temwa
-nyorwa	chopped/hit
-nzwa	feel
-ona	see
-onana	see each other
-onda	thin
-ondoroka	lose weight
-ongorora	examine
-onwa	seen (passive)
-ora	bad/rotten
-pa	give
-panana	give each other
-patsanura	separate
-pedza	finish
-pedziswa	finished by
-pera izwi	be hoarse
-pesana	lose touch with each other
-peta	fold
-petwa	folded
-pfeka	wear
-pfura	shoot/pass

-pfurana	shoot/pass each other
-pinda	enter
-pindura mibvunzo	tackle questions
-pomba	pump
-pomera	accuse
-pora	heal/cool down
-pukuta	wipe/clean
-pukuta	wipe/clean with a cloth
-punza	break
-punzwa	broken (passive)
-pusa	easy
-puta	smoke
-putsa	knock down
-rambidza	disallow
-rapwa	be healed
-rara	sleep
-rarama	survive/live
-rasa	throw away/lose
-rasika	get lost
-ratidzika	to appear [as being something]
-rayiwa	get slaughtered
-redza	fish
-regerewa	be forgiven
-rera	raise [young ones]
-rera vana	child spacing
-rima	plough
-rira	sing/crow
-rize	sting/bite
-rodha	load
-rodzwa	be sharpened
-rova	hit
-rovana	hit each other
-rumbidza	to praise
-runga	stir
-rutsa	vomit
-rwadza ne	in pain of [something]
-rwadzwa ne	to be in pain of [something, eg stomach]
-rwara	sick
-rwisana	fight one another
-sada kudya	loss of appetite

-sakura	weed with an implement
-sara	remain
-sarudza	choose
-sefa	sieve
-seka	laugh
-sekana	laugh at each other
-shamisika	surprise/shock
-shanya	visit
-shata	bad/rotten/ugly
-shaya hope	be sleepless
-shingirira	persevere
-shupika	find difficult
-shushikana	worry
-simudza	lift/raise
-sonera	sew
-sunda	push
-sunga	tie
-sunungura	untie
-sviba	get dirty
-svika	arrive
-swatuka	straight
-tadza	fail
-tadza kubudirira	fail to succeed
-takura	carry
-takurana	carry each other
-tamba	play
-tambisa	waste
-tambudza	cause suffering
-tambura	writhe with agony/anguish
-tandarira	socialize
-tanga	start
-tarisa	look at
-taura	speak
-tema	cut
-temwa	cut (passive)
-tenda	thank
-tendekana	faithful
-tengesa	sell
-tengesana	sell each other [out]
-ti	say

-tiler	tile
-tiza	flee
-tonhora	cold
-tora	taken
-torwa	taken
-tsanangura	explain
-tsinga	hurt/cripple
-tsvuka	be red/ripe
-tuka	scold
-tukana	scold each other
-tuma	send
-tumana	send each other
-tumbura	lance/spike
-tumidza	call something [some name]
-tungidza	strike a match/light a fire
-tya	afraid
-tyoka	break
-unganidza	stack/pile
-uraya nekumhanya	to kill by running
-vaka	build
-vakwa	built (passive)
-vhota	vote
-vimba	hope
-vimbika	be trustworthy
-wacha	wash (in a washing machine or by hand)
-wanza	top up
-wedzera masimba	empower
-wina	win
-wirirana	agree with one another
-zadza	fill up
-zora	apply [ointment/grease/etc]
-zvekusima	transplant (plant material)
-zviuraya	kill oneself (ie commit suicide)
amai	mother
asi	but
baba	father
badza	hoe
bakwa	wood pile
bandeji	bandage
bato	political party

bazi	branch (of a tree)
bepanhau	newspaper
bhaketi	bucket
bhande	belt
bhapu	lungs
bhaudi	bolt
bhururutswa	to be blown
bofu	blind person
boka	team
buri	hole
bvudzi	hair
chando	cold
changamire	sir
chara	finger
chero	so long/since
chidembo	civet cat
chidhina	brick
chidimbu	piece [of something]
chido	something wanted or desirable
chidyamatoo	a meat eater
chidzidzo	lesson
chigaro	chair
chigero	shaver
chikosoro	nasal cough
chimbuzi	toilet
chimufananidzo	statue
chinamato	prayer
chindevere	Ndebele language
chingwa	bread
chinhu	thing
chinonakidza	an interesting thing
chipatara	hospital
chipembere	rhino
chipfuva	chest cough
chipikiri	nail
chipo	gift
chirambakuudzwa	a person who refuses advice
chiredzo	fishing hook
chiremba	doctor
chirimwa	crop

chironda	wound
chiroto	dream
chisetso	something laughed at
chisi	something that isn't yours
chiso	face
chitengo	something bought
chiteshi	station
chitima	train
chitoro	store
chitsigiro	supporting structure
chitsvairiswa	broom
chivezwa	carving
chivhitivhiti	television
chiziviso	announcement
chizivo	something known
chokwadi	truth
chombo	weapon
dama	cheek
dambudziko	problem
danga	kraal
dhakwa	drunk
dhorobha	town
dhura	expensive
diki	small (adjective)
domasi	tomato
dombo	rock
doro	beer
dumbu	stomach/intestines
dumbu	stomach
dzinde	cutting [from a tree/shrub]
dzivirira pamuviri	birth control
dziya	warm
dzungu	dizziness
fafitera	window
fodya	tobacco
foshoro	shovel
fumo (auxillary)	early in the morning
futi	also
ganda	skin
garaji	garage

garo (auxillary)	always
girizi	grease
gobvu	thick
gomba	ditch
gomo	mountain
gondo	eagle
gonzo	rat
gore	year
gore rakapera	last year
gore roga roga	each and every year
gotsi	back of the head
grass	uswa
grovo	glove
gudo	baboon
gumbezi	blanket
gumbo	leg
guru	big (adjective)
hanga	guineafowl
hanya	care
hari	clay pot
hari	traditional clay pot
hoe	badza
hove	fish
howa	mushroom
huchi	honey
huku	chicken
huma	forehead
hunhu	code of conduct
huori	corruption
hupenyu	life
hupfumi	hupfumi
huro	throat
huwandu	quantity
hwahwa	alcohol
hwanda	hide
imba	house
imba	house
Inda	louse
ivai nechokwadi kuti...	make sure that...
iyoni	iron

jaya	young man
jekiseni	injection
Jira	cloth/fabric
jira	cloth
jongwe	cockerel
kana	if/or/when/even
kandiro	small plate
kanzura	counsellor
kapeti	carpet
kazhumu	goat's beard
kitsi	cat
kiyenura	unlock
ku	to/at
kuchengetedza zvakanaka	to maintain well
kune rimwi divi	on the one hand/on the other hand
kunze	outside
kupisa muviri	run a temperature (when ill)
kusabhadhara	without paying
kushomeka kwemvura	deyhydration
kutsi	deep
kuvapo kwangu	my existence
kwese kwese	everywhere
mabonzo	bones
maburi	holes
madandemutande	cobwebs
madziro	walls
madziva	fast flowing rivers
mafaro	entertainments
magaro	soot
magetsi	electricity
magirazi	spectacles
maiwe	expression of surprise or shock
majuru	termites
makonye	bacteria
makunguo	crows
mamiriro ezvinhu	situation
manenji	unexpected happening
manje manje	shortly (slang)
manyoka	diarrhoea
manyowa	manure

marara	rubbish
mararia	malaria
marimwezuro	day before yesterday
mariva	traps
maruva	flowers
mashandisiro	workings
mashizha	leaves
Masimba	strengths
matadza	gums
mbabvu	rib
mbada	leopard
mbambaira	sweet potatoes
mbavha	thief
mbereko	cradle
mberi	in front of/forward
mbeu	seed
mbeva	mouse
mbiro	warning
mbo (auxillary)	once, ever or never
mbonje	deep impact wound
mbudzana	young goat
mbudzi	goat
mechanica	mechanic
mhanya mhanya	run about
mhanza	luck
mhara	impala
mhepo	wind
mhosva	a wrong/crime
mhuka	animal
mhuru	calf
miganhu	borders
mota	boil
moyo	heart
mu	in
mubairo	medal
mubatsiri	helper
mucheche	baby
muchero	fruit
mudhudhudhu	motorbike
mudhuri	wall

mudzi	root
mudzidzi	student
muenzi	visitor
mufambi	traveller
mugoni	an expert
mugwagwa	road
muhomba – flower bed	flower bed
muhoro	salary
mukadzi	woman
mukaka	milk
mukatikati memwoyo wangu	in my heart of hearts
mukomana	boy
mukuru	elder
mukurumbira	fame
mumhanyi	runner
muna nyamavhuvhu	in August
munamati	one who prays
muningina	small brother
mupurisa	policeman
muredzi	fisherman
murimi	farmer
muripo	fine (cash)
muriwo	vegetables
muromo	mouth
murume	man
murwere	sick person
musana	back/spine
musangano	meeting
museve	arrow
musevenzi	worker
mushonga	medicine/chemicals
mushure me	after
musikana	girl
musoja	soldier
musoro	head
mutambo	game
mutambudziki	one who suffers
mutanda	log
mutapi wenhau	journalist

mutemo	law
mutengesi	shop keeper
muti	tree
mutsvairi	sweeper
mutungamiriri	leader
muvaki	builder
muvimbi	someone trustworthy
muvimbiki	trustworthy person
muviri	body
mvumo	permission
mvura	water
mvuu	hippopatamous
mwaka we chando	winter
mwaka wechando wakapera	last winter
mwanasikana	daughter
mwedzi	month
mwedzi wakapera	last month
mwenje	light
nandare yenhabvu	soccer pitch
ndebvu	beard
ndege	aeroplane
ndiro	plate
ndo (auxillary)	in order to
ne ku	and [referring to places] or via [some place]
ne/na	and/by/with
nekuda kwa	because of [insert reason]
nekudaro	hence/therefore
nekuti/pamusoro pe	because
nepkeni	napkin
nezve	about
ngo (auxillary)	simply
ngura	rust
nguruve	pig
nhabvu	soccer
nhamo	poverty
nhanga	pumpkin
nharo	argument
nhasi	today
nhata	aphid
nhembwe	duiker

nhondo	seedling
nhondo	seedlings
nhoroondo	history
nhunzi	fly
nyama	meat
nyamunatsi	kind/good person
nyamutsingwa	injured person
nyango/kana hazvo/kanapo	although/even though/despite/inspite of
nyanzvi	expert
nyenyedzi	stars
nyika	land
nyoka	snake
nzeve	ears
nzou	elephant
nzvimbo	place
onyeni	onion
pa	on/at
pachipamwe	informal hello
padhuze ne	close to
pakati pe	in the middle of
pakati peusiku	in the middle of the night
pakupedzisira	finally or "to finish"
pamberi pe	in front of
pamhidzira	add (can be used interchangeably with "wedzera")
panguva iyo	at that time
panguva iyoyo	at that time
pashure pe	behind
pazasi pe	beneath
pedyo ne	close to
pfunde	sorghum
pfupi	short (adjective)
pick	piki
pinjisi	pliers
piritsi	pill
ponji	puncture
priest	muparidzi
pump	pombi
pundutso	advantage (noun)
purazi	commercial farm

refu	tall (adjective)
rima	darkness
rimwe	another (hard sounding conjugation)
ropa	blood
ruchengetedzo	maintenance
rudzi	species or variety
rufu	death
rugare	peace/luxury
rukudzo	respect
ruredzo	fishing techniques/methods
rurimi	tongue
rusununguko	freedom
rutambudzo	system causing suffering
ruvimbiko	loyalty
ruzha	noise
ruzivo	knowledge
rwizi	river
saka	so
sango	forest
sekerera	smile
sekuti	for example
sevisi	service
sezvo	since
shakata	fruit (ofa particular wild variety)
shanwari	friend
shiri	bird
shoma	small quantity
shuffle	foshoro
shuga	sugar
shumba	lion
simudza	lift up
sipho	soap
siyana siyana	different
sora	weeds
svondo rinouya	next week
tadza kuita weti	difficulty urinating
tafura	table
tambo	rope
tete	aunt
to (auxillary)	already

tsamba	letter
tsaona	accident
tsika	customs
tsoko	vervet monkey
tsuro	rabbit
tsva (adjective)	new
tukana	mutually shout at or scold
tuma	send
twiza	giraffe
urema	disability
urwa	puss
utachiwana	bacteria
utano	health
utsanana	hygiene
vara guru	capital letter
varwi	fighters
vhiki	week
vhiki rakapera	last week
vhiri	wheel
vhuvhuta	wind
wanzo (auxillary)	frequently/often
waya	wire
yusa	US dollar
zadzisa	fulfill
zai	egg
zhinji	a lot
zo (auxillary)	finally
zororo	holidays
zumbuko	crossing place
zuva	day
zvakakosha kuti	it's important [to do...]
zvakawanda	plentiful
zvinogoneka	it is possible
zvipanera	spanners
zvipfuyo	livestock
zvirimwa	plants
zviroto	dreams
zvisina njodzi	safely (literally: without danger)
zvitsiko	footprints
zvivakiso	building materials

ENGLISH – SHONA

abortion	-bvisa pamuviri
about	nezve
accept	-bvuma
accident	tsaona
accuse	-pomera
add (used interchangeably with "wedzera")	pamhidzira
advantage (noun)	pundutso
aeroplane	ndege
afraid	-tya
after	mushure me
agree with one another	-wirirana
alcohol	hwahwa
alot	zhinji
already	to (auxillary)
also	futi
although/even though/despite/inspite of	nyango/kana hazvo/kanapo
always	garo (auxillary)
an expert	mugoni
an interesting thing	chinonakidza
and [when referring to places] or via [some place]	ne ku
and/by/with	ne/na
animal	mhuka
announcement	chiziviso
another (hard sounding conjugation)	rimwe
aphid	nhata
apply [ointment/grease/etc]	-zora
argue with one another	-kakavadzana
argument	nharo
arrive	-svika
arrow	museve
at that time	panguva iyo
at that time	panguva iyoyo
aunt	tete
baboon	gudo
baby	mucheche
back of the head	gotsi
back/spine	musana

bacteria	makonye
bacteria	utachiwana
bad/rotten	-ora
bad/rotten/ugly	-shata
badza	hoe
bandage	bandeji
be choked	-dzipwa
be forgiven	-regerewa
be healed	-rapwa
be hoarse	-pera izwi
be picked	-nhongwa
be red/ripe	-tsvuka
be sharpened	-rodzwa
be sleepless	-shaya hope
be trustworthy	-vimbika
beard	ndebvu
because	nekuti/pamusoro pe
because of [insert reason]	nekuda kwa
beer	doro
behind	pashure pe
belt	bhande
beneath	pazasi pe
big (adjective)	guru
bird	shiri
birth control	dzivirira pamuviri
blanket	gumbezi
blind person	bofu
blood	ropa
body	muviri
boil	mota
bolt	bhaudi
bones	mabonzo
borders	miganhu
bother	-netsa
bother each other	-netsana
bothered by	-netswa
boy	mukomana
braai/barbecue/roast	-gotcha

branch (of a tree)	bazi
bread	chingwa
break	-punza
break	-tyoka
breathe	-fema
brick	chidhina
broken	-chekwa
broken (passive)	-punzwa
broom	chitsvairiswa
bucket	bhaketi
build	-vaka
builder	muvaki
building materials	zvivakiso
built (passive)	-vakwa
bump	-dhuma
bump into each other	-dhumana
but	asi
calf	mhuru
call	-daidza
call something [some name]	-tumidza
capital letter	vara guru
care	hanya
carpet	kapeti
carry	-takura
carry each other	-takurana
carving	chivezwa
cat	kitsi
cause	-konzera
cause	-konzeresa
cause suffering	-tambudza
chair	chigaro
chase	-dzinga
chase	-dzingirira
cheek	dama
chest cough	chipfuva
chicken	huku
child spacing	-rera vana
choose	-sarudza
chopped/hit	-nyorwa
civet cat	chidembo

clay pot	hari
clever (used statively)	-ngwara
climb	-kwira
close to	padhuze ne
close to	pedyo ne
cloth	jira
cloth/fabric	Jira
cobwebs	madandemutande
cockerel	jongwe
code of conduct	hunhu
cold	-tonhora
cold	chando
commercial farm	purazi
cook	-bika
corruption	huori
counsellor	kanzura
cradle	mbereko
crash into	-dumira
crash into each other	-dhumana
crop	chirimwa
crossing place	zumbuko
crows	makunguo
cry	-chema
customs	tsika
cut	-tema
cut (passive)	-temwa
cutting [from a tree/shrub]	dzinde
darkness	rima
daughter	mwanasikana
day	zuva
day before yesterday	marimwezuro
death	rufu
deep	kutsi
deep impact wound	mbonje
deepen	-dzikise
deyhydration	kushomeka kwemvura
diarrhoea	manyoka
different	siyana siyana
difficulty urinating	tadza kuita weti
disability	urema

disallow	-rambidza
ditch	gomba
dizziness	dzungu
do [to] each other	-itirana
doctor	chiremba
dream	chiroto
dreams	zviroto
drive	-draiva
drunk	dhakwa
dry	-nanikai
duiker	nhembwe
each and every year	gore roga roga
eagle	gondo
early in the morning	fumo (auxillary)
ears	nzeve
easy	-pusa
egg	zai
elder	mukuru
electricity	magetsi
elephant	nzou
embarress	-nyadzisa
empower	-wedzera masimba
enough	-kwana
enter	-pinda
entertainments	mafaro
everywhere	kwese kwese
examine	-ongorora
expensive	dhura
expert	nyanzvi
expire	-expaya
explain	-tsanangura
expression of surprise or shock	maiwe
extinguish [fire]	-dzimura
face	chiso
fail	-kundikana
fail	-tadza
fail to succeed	-tadza kubudirira
faithful	-tendekana
fall	-donha
fall	-kundikana

fame	mukurumbira
farmer	murimi
fast flowing rivers	madziva
father	baba
feed	-gutsa
feel	-nzwa
fight one another	-rwisana
fighters	varwi
fill up	-zadza
finally	zo (auxillary)
finally or "to finish"	pakupedzisira
find difficult	-shupika
fine (cash)	muripo
finger	chara
finish	-pedza
finished by	-pedziswa
fish	hove
fish	-redza
fisherman	muredzi
fishing hook	chiredzo
fishing techniques/methods	ruredzo
flee	-tiza
flower bed	muhomba – flower bed
flowers	maruva
fly	-bhururuka
fly	nhunzi
fold	-peta
folded	-petwa
footprints	zvitsiko
for example	sekuti
forehead	huma
forest	sango
forget	-kanganwa
foshoro	shuffle
freedom	rusununguko
frequently/often	wanzo (auxillary)
friend	shanwari
fruit	muchero
fruit (ofa particular wild variety)	shakata
fulfill	zadzisa

game	mutambo
garage	garaji
get dirty	-sviba
get lost	-rasika
get slaughtered	-rayiwa
get stabbed	-bayiwa
gift	chipo
giraffe	twiza
girl	musikana
give	-pa
give each other	-panana
glove	grovo
go	-enda
goat	mbudzi
goat's beard	kazhumu
good	-naka
grease	girizi
greet	-mhoresa
greet each other	-mhoresana
grow	-kura
grow/germinate	-mera
guineafowl	hanga
gums	matadza
hair	bvudzi
head	musoro
heal/cool down	-pora
health	utano
heart	moyo
help	-batsira
help each other	-batsirana
helper	mubatsiri
hence/therefore	nekudaro
hide	hwanda
hippopatamous	mvuu
history	nhoroondo
hit	-rova
hit each other	-rovana
hoe	badza
hold/catch	-bata
hole	buri

holes	maburi
holidays	zororo
honey	huchi
hope	-vimba
hospital	chipatara
house	imba
house	imba
hupfumi	hupfumi
hurt/cripple	-tsinga
hygiene	utsanana
if/or/when/even	kana
impala	mhara
in	mu
in August	muna nyamavhuvhu
in front of	pamberi pe
in front of/forward	mberi
in my heart of hearts	mukatikati memwoyo wangu
in order to	ndo (auxillary)
in pain of [something]	-rwadza ne
in the middle of	pakati pe
in the middle of the night	pakati peusiku
informal hello	pachipamwe
injection	jekiseni
injured by	-kuvadzwa
injured person	nyamutsingwa
interest	-nakidza
iron	-aina
iron	iyoni
it is possible	zvinogoneka
it's important [to do...]	Zvakakosha kuti
journalist	mutapi wenhau
keep/look after	-chengetedza
kill oneself (ie commit suicide)	-zviuraya
kind/good person	nyamunatsi
knock down	-putsa
knowledge	ruzivo
kraal	danga
lance/spike	-tumbura
land	-mhara
land	nyika

last month	mwedzi wakapera
last week	vhiki rakapera
last winter	mwaka wechando wakapera
last year	gore rakapera
laugh	-seka
laugh at each other	-sekana
law	mutemo
leader	mutungamiriri
learn	-dzidza
leaves	mashizha
leg	gumbo
leopard	mbada
lesson	chidzidzo
letter	tsamba
life	hupenyu
lift up	simudza
lift/raise	-simudza
light	mwenje
lion	shumba
livestock	zvipfuyo
load	-rodha
lock	-kiya – lock
log	mutanda
look at	-tarisa
lose touch with each other	-pesana
lose weight	-ondoroka
loss of appetite	-sada kudya
louse	inda
loyalty	ruvimbiko
luck	mhanza
lungs	bhapu
maintenance	ruchengetedzo
make level	-enzana
make sure that...	ivai nechokwadi kuti...
malaria	mararia
man	murume
manure	manyowa
meat	nyama
meat eater	chidyamatoo
mechanic	mechanica

medal	mubairo
medicine/chemicals	mushonga
meeting	musangano
milk	mukaka
miscarriage	-bva pamuviri
miss each other	-fungana
month	mwedzi
mother	amai
motorbike	mudhudhudhu
mountain	gomo
mouse	mbeva
mouth	muromo
muparidzi	priest
mushroom	howa
mutually shout at or scold	tukana
my existence	kuvapo kwangu
nail	chipikiri
napkin	nepkeni
nasal cough	chikosoro
Ndebele language	chindevere
new	tsva (adjective)
newspaper	bepanhau
next week	svondo rinouya
noise	ruzha
on the one hand/on the other hand	kune rimwi divi
on/at	pa
once, ever or never	mbo (auxillary)
one who prays	munamati
one who suffers	mutambudziki
onion	onyeni
outside	kunze
pay	-badhara
peace/luxury	rugare
permission	mvumo
permit [something to happen]	-bvumidza
persevere	-shingirira
person who refuses advice	chirambakuudzwa
pick up	-nonga
piece [of something]	chidimbu
pig	nguruve

piki	pick
pill	piritsi
place	nzvimbo
plant seeds	-dyara
plants	zvirimwa
plate	ndiro
play	-tamba
plentiful	zvakawanda
pliers	pinjisi
plough	-rima
pluck by hand	-dzura
policeman	mupurisa
political party	bato
pombi	pump
poverty	nhamo
pray	-namata
prayer	chinamato
press	-dzvinya
problem	dambudziko
protect	-dzivirira
pull	-donza
pull	-donza
pump	-pomba
pumpkin	nhanga
puncture	ponji
punzwa	-cheka
push	-sunda
puss	urwa
quantity	huwandu
rabbit	tsuro
raise [young ones]	-rera
rat	gonzo
reduce	-dzika
remain	-sara
respect	rukudzo
return [something]	-dzosera
rhino	chipembere
rib	mbabvu
river	rwizi
road	mugwagwa

rock	dombo
root	mudzi
rope	tambo
rubbish	marara
run a temperature (when ill)	kupisa muviri
run about	mhanya mhanya
runner	mumhanyi
running stomach	-chaya
rush	-mhanya-mhanya
rust	ngura
safely (literally: without danger)	zvisina njodzi
salary	muhoro
say	-ti
scold	-tuka
scold each other	-tukana
scrape	-marwa
see	-ona
see each other	-onana
seed	mbeu
seedling	nhondo
seedlings	nhondo
seen (passive)	-onwa
sell	-tengesa
sell each other [out]	-tengesana
send	-tuma
send	tuma
send each other	-tumana
separate	-patsanura
service	sevisi
sew	-sonera
shake	-bvunda
shave	-gera
shaver	chigero
shepherd [back somewhere]	-dzora
shoot/pass	-pfura
shoot/pass each other	-pfurana
shop keeper	mutengesi
short (adjective)	pfupi
shortly (slang)	manje manje
shovel	foshoro

sick	-rwara
sick person	murwere
sieve	-sefa
simply	ngo (auxillary)
since	sezvo
sing/crow	-rira
sir	changamire
situation	mamiriro ezvinhu
skin	ganda
sleep	-rara
small (adjective)	diki
small brother	muningina
small plate	kandiro
small quantity	shoma
smell [like something]	-nhuwa
smile	sekerera
smoke	-puta
snake	nyoka
so	saka
so long/since	chero
soap	sipho
soccer	nhabvu
soccer pitch	nandare yenhabvu
socialize	-tandarira
soldier	musoja
someone trustworthy	muvimbi
something bought	chitengo
something known	chizivo
something laughed at	chisetso
something that isn't yours	chisi
something wanted or desirable	chido
soot	magaro
sorghum	pfunde
spanners	zvipanera
speak	-taura
species or variety	rudzi
spectacles	magirazi
stack/pile	-unganidza
stars	nyenyedzi
start	-tanga

station	chiteshi
statue	chimufananidzo
steal	-ba
sting/bite	-rize
stir	-runga
stolen	-biwa
stomach	dumbu
stomach/intestines	dumbu
stop	-misa
store	chitoro
straight	-swatuka
strengths	Masimba
strike a match/light a fire	-tungidza
student	mudzidzi
stutter	-kakama
succeed	-budirira
sugar	shuga
supporting structure	chitsigiro
surprise/shock	-shamisika
survive/live	-rarama
sweeper	mutsvairi
sweet potatoes	mbambaira
system causing suffering	rutambudzo
table	tafura
tackle questions	-pindura mibvunzo
taken	-tora
taken	-torwa
tall (adjective)	refu
teach	-dzidzisa
teach each other	-dzidzisana
team	boka
television	chivhitivhiti
temwa	-nyora
termites	majuru
thank	-tenda
thick	-kora
thick	gobvu
thief	mbavha
thin	-onda
thing	chinhu

think/miss	-funga
throat	huro
throw	-kanda
throw away/lose	-rasa
tie	-sunga
tile	-tiler
to appear [as being something]	-ratidzika
to be blown	bhururutswa
to be in pain of [something, eg stomach]	-rwadzwa ne
to kill by running	-uraya nekumhanya
to maintain well	kuchengetedza zvakanaka
to praise	-rumbidza
to reduce/shrink	-dzikira
to respect	-kudza
to respect each other	-kudzana
to/at	ku
tobacco	fodya
today	nhasi
toilet	chimbuzi
tomato	domasi
tongue	rurimi
top up	-wanza
touch one another	-gumana
town	dhorobha
traditional clay pot	hari
train	chitima
transplant (plant material)	-zvekusima
traps	mariva
traveller	mufambi
tree	muti
trustworthy person	muvimbiki
truth	chokwadi
unexpected happening	manenji
unlock	kiyenura
untie	-sunungura
US dollar	yusa
uswa	grass
vegetables	muriwo
vervet monkey	tsoko
visit	-shanya

visitor	muenzi
vomit	-rutsa
vote	-vhota
wall	mudhuri
walls	madziro
warm	dziya
warning	mbiro
wash	-geza
wash (in a washing machine or by hand)	-wacha
wash each other	-gezana
waste	-tambisa
water	mvura
water/irrigate	-diridza
weapon	chombo
wear	-pfeka
weed with an implement	-sakura
weeds	sora
week	vhiki
wheel	vhiri
win	-wina
wind	mhepo
wind	vhuvhuta
window	fafitera
winter	mwaka we chando
wipe/clean	-pukuta
wipe/clean with a cloth	-pukuta
wire	waya
without paying	kusabhadhara
woman	mukadzi
wood pile	bakwa
work with each other	-batana
worker	musevenzi
workings	mashandisiro
worry	-shushikana
wound	chironda
writhe with agony/anguish	-tambura
wrongdoing or crime	mhosva
year	gore
young goat	mbudzana
young man	jaya